never
say
never

Give Glory and
praise to God
and delight in
His goodness.

Rhonda
Sanders

never
say
never

Rhonda Sanders

Tate Publishing & Enterprises

Published by Tate Publishing & Enterprises, LLC
127 E. Trade Center Terrace | Mustang, Oklahoma 73064 USA
1.888.361.9473 | www.tatepublishing.com

Tate Publishing is committed to excellence in the publishing industry. The company reflects the philosophy established by the founders, based on Psalm 68:11,
"The Lord gave the word and great was the company of those who published it."

Book design copyright © 2010 by Tate Publishing, LLC. All rights reserved.
Cover design by Scott Parrish
Interior design by Nathan Harmony

Published in the United States of America

ISBN: 978-1-61663-713-2
1. Religion / Christian Life / Inspirational
2. Religion / Christian Life / Personal Growth
10.06.03

Dedication

I'd like to dedicate this book to my husband and our seven children, Dawn, Randy 2, John, Michael, Tommy, Ashley, and Garry.

And to our grandchildren, whose names I won't list because we feel that there will be more in the future, and we don't want to leave even one out.

To my husband, Randy, who has been so supportive during the writing process, always encouraging when it was needed, and who lived through some of the issues created by joining our lives together in the midst of this book's birthing process. I love you and thank God for you daily.

To my children—all of you have a special place in my heart. I could never have made it this far without having you in my life. You are my heart.

To my grandchildren, you are the bomb. Nothing in life is more joy giving than you guys. I love all of you so very much. Each different personality and different quirk is so special.

Acknowledgments

This book is not my story; it's God's grace shown to me through my life up to this point. It is dependent on God's continued love and grace in my life. Thank God we have his Word to guide us in our lives, and we can be encouraged that he already knows what we need. He wants to enter into a serious relationship with us.

I'd like to express special thanks to Leo Free, who was my pastor several years ago. Leo is the one person who told me to write my story and get it published, and he continued to tell me to do it for years. I finally took his advice, and whether it sells one book or more, it's a wonderful release. Thanks, Leo. You knew what you were talking about. You had faith in me. More than that, you were my pastor and a stand-in father to my children at a time when they really needed you. That means a lot. You are a forever friend.

My friend Mary Strain, thank you for helping me by reading and editing the first book, *Journey of Love* and this new one. You are an amazing woman and such an inspiration to me. When I grow up, I want to be like you as much as God allows me to be and still be myself.

Table of Contents

Never Say Never

What's the first thing you think of when someone says, "Never"? I love to read and study meanings of the words I read. I like to know different ways a word is used. Never means not ever. Never is used liberally throughout our language.

When I first encountered a baby's dirty diaper, my first verbalization was, "Oh, God, I am *never* going to have a baby if that's what it's like." Never say "never"; I had three of my own.

When we first experience something negative, sometimes it is natural for our reaction to be saying "never." I *never* want to do that again; I *never* want to go out on a date with that guy or gal again; or I am *never* going to drink again—whatever the activity may be.

God gave me the title for this book some time ago, and I have since had it verified to me in various methods, time and time again. I allowed it to bounce around at the back of my mind for several months; I was waiting for God to give me the rest of the book to go with the title. Usually, though, once I start writing, I listen to God, and the writing starts and takes on life and flows without having to wait on it. God had already given me the data for this book, and now I am finally able to put it on paper.

I used to use "never" a lot more than I do now. I was in a place in my life where I wanted to give up on the hope of any kind of marital relationship being sincere; I decided to totally give up any hope in that area. My famous last words were, "I'll *never* get married again."

Well, God disproved that one when I met my wonderful husband. God allowed me to understand the difference between a partnership and a marital relationship. For the first time in my forty-plus years, God favored me with a loving and gentle husband and taught me what a marriage is supposed to be like. In the process of learning this lesson, I began to understand more about God's love and how to have a relationship with God.

Since then, I have been known to use a few "nevers," but not nearly as frequently or as carelessly as before. Now, I at least attempt to pay more attention to those words, which I formerly carelessly tossed about. Now I try to never say "never."

Did you know that words like *never* and *always* are absolutes in the English language? In Webster's Dictionary, the word *absolute* means "unconditional." If someone uses the word *never*, they are saying that under no condition will they change the action or behavior being discussed. Using words like *never* and *always* in arguments don't leave much room for discussion of the subject in question. A lot of arguments could be prevented if we learn not to use these two words in an accusatory manner whenever we are trying to communicate with a loved one or a coworker. Why? If someone tells you that you *never* pick up your clothes, you feel that they didn't appreciate it the one time you did pick up your clothes, so why bother anymore, right?

These two words are used in accusatory ways in arguments between loved ones. Do you suppose that if we could learn to substitute "I feel like" or "It seems to me" in place of the "never" or "always" that the same statement could sound less accusatory? Let's see.

I *feel* like you don't pick up your clothes on a regular basis. *It seems to me* that you don't pick up your clothes on a regular basis. It is basically saying the same thing; however, by simply changing a few words you change accusatory tone to one that is less threatening to the other person. An argument would be less likely to ensue if these slight changes in language were made during the course of the conversation.

If we were to substitute the word *sometimes* in place of the *never* or *always*, it could develop into a preventative measure and redirect an argument into more useful discussion. This should also indicate to us how careful we should be when talking to others, especially when we are in a position to hurt or encourage someone else. When we try to convince someone to see our point of view, it is important to give them a choice. The other person will not feel boxed in if you leave out the limiting words *never* and *always* in support of your argument.

God is still in control, and he is still in the miracle business. My husband and I attend a church that is a mix of different churches—a little bit gospel, a little bit rock and roll, a little bit of all different varieties of people. There are rich and poor, people of different religious backgrounds, people from different walks of life, people in different stages of faith, and people of different races. It is a down-to-earth church with a wonderful and loving fellowship. We are a Bible-believing church family who believes that God still does miracles today.

We have some friends who truly need miracles in their lives, and we—the entire church family—believe God will perform these miracles on their behalf. God is no respecter of persons, so we expect him to do great and wondrous things in the lives of the people we lift up to him in prayer.

We have one friend who was recently diagnosed with Crohn's disease, Parkinson's disease, and several other medical complications. She has gone before our church family and let us all know that she is expecting a miracle from God in her health issues. When we discussed her prayer needs, she told me specifically not to pray for her to get better, but to pray for a miracle. It has been prophesied over the body of Christ in our fellowship that this part of the church body would have a documented miracle, and my friend is claiming that miracle.

Some people do not understand that kind of faith, yet we all have it. The difference is in exercising it. Just like our bodies, our faith grows stronger through exercise. Use it or lose it.

You may have heard the truism that people will look at a glass of water that is half-filled, and some people will say it is half-empty and others will say it is half-full. Which one do you want to be? Yes, reality is a place where we all have to live and be aware of how things apply to our lives realistically. However, we also need to stretch our faith by exercising it and allowing ourselves to believe in God's words to us in his Bible.

Miracles are not just something of the past; they happen on earth all the time. Maybe we aren't looking for them, so it makes it harder to see them. Some major examples of miracles for me are children. Every birth is a miracle from God and a wonderful gift. Being able to look into that tiny little face and see some resemblance to either parent, grandparent, or sibling is a miracle to me. God forms each child within its mother's womb (Isaiah 49:1–5 which reads, "Listen, O isles, unto me; and hearken, ye people, from far; The Lord hath called me from the womb; from the bowels of my mother hath he made mention of my name. And he hath made my mouth like a sharp sword; in the shadow of his hand hath he hid me, and made me a polished shaft; in his quiver hath he hid me; And said unto me, Thou art my servant, O Israel, in whom I will be glorified. Then I said, 'I have laboured in vain, I have spent my strength for nought, and in vain; yet surely my judgment is with the Lord, and my work with my God.' And now, saith the Lord that formed me from the womb to be his servant, to bring Jacob again to him, 'Though Israel be not gathered, yet shall I be glorious in the eyes of the Lord, and my God shall be my strength'" KJV). Each little human being is a miracle. The growth of that baby into infanthood, throughout the adolescent years, the teens (oh, boy) and into adulthood is a huge miracle. Life itself is a miracle and a gift to be appreciated each day.

In 2004, we lost a young friend at our home church. He was the same age as my daughter, twenty years old. He and my daughter attended school together and were good friends. His life touched so many others, not only within our church family but also in the community. The memory of his loving spirit will remain with us forever. His life was a powerful example for us that we have no promises for tomorrow and that we should be thankful for the miracle of life each day. It should also remind us that we are to live that life for Christ every day, in every way possible.

This young friend did just that. He lived life to the fullest every day and sometimes lived it on the edge. I suspect that he did not let much in life slide by him. He was involved in many activities and seemed to enjoy life so much. I believe he looked at adversity as a challenge rather than a burden. He was helpful to his friends who needed help and was deeply involved in their lives. He had accountability with other young people regarding his Christian life. I would like to be like this young friend and be able to look adversity in the face and consider it a challenge, one that I intend to get through with the help of God. What about you? Wouldn't you prefer to accept the challenges rather than be burdened down with stress?

When I discussed the birth of this book with some friends recently—how God had confirmed the name of the book for me—I met some surprise and a little amusement from them. Some commented that it was a catchphrase, and others did not seem to understand the phrase, yet it was what I felt Gold was teaching me at the time. Never say never because nothing is impossible for God. Never put a limit on God and what he can and will do in people's lives. He is sovereign, and I believe he is telling each of us today to not give up on our faith. Don't speak the *never* word when you are speaking about your own life. We each have different paths to follow, yet God is capable of leading each of us—individually and collectively—on our walks with him.

For several years I was a single mom with many responsibilities. Even when I was married for short periods in between times of being single, it seemed that the financial responsibility for the family fell on me. For a long time this bothered me because of my upbringing in the church I attended growing up. We were taught that the man was the head of the household and, as such, the breadwinner, and that the woman was the homemaker.

However, at times it became my responsibility to feed and clothe my children and provide a home for them. One way to look at is that I did not have the faith to wait on

God to be the provider. Believe me, Satan tried hard to oppress me with thoughts that I was in the wrong place and doing the wrong thing or that I was not a good mom because I was working instead of being at home with my children 24/7. Yet I knew that it was my job to do the best that I could to provide for my children, and the only way I knew to do that was to take a job outside of our home.

There are verses in the Bible that will guide us to our destiny if we allow them. There is one that I kept going back to when Satan tried to impress on my mind that I was wrong to be working outside the home, and that verse refers to being an infidel if you are not willing to work to provide for your family. First Timothy 5:8 says, "But if any provide not for his own, and specially for those of his own house, he hath denied the faith, and is worse than an infidel." I went back and forth with Satan, until finally God gave me peace through the counseling of a pastor friend. He pointed out to me something that I knew—God was the head of my household and the Father of my children. He reminded me that even though I was trying so hard to be both mom and dad to those gifts he had placed in my life, God was their Father. God was not going to desert them or me.

That gave me peace, and I was able to resolve that issue and place my faith in God that he was going to help raise my children. He gave me the assurance that they would be provided for emotionally, physically, and in every other way.

God doesn't lie, and he doesn't change. If he performed miracles in the time the Bible was penned, why wouldn't he do miracles for us today too? I think our disbelief keeps us from seeing the manifestation of more miracles in our daily lives. Satan encourages us to be apathetic; it's his job to steal, kill, and destroy our lives if we allow him to do so. Satan wants us to be down, depressed, disgusted with our lives so that he can deceive us into believing there is no such thing as a loving Father who cares so much about us—even the small details in our lives. If we cannot believe in a loving Father God, we cannot believe God would be willing to perform miracles in our lives. Not being able to believe in miracles keeps us from seeing the everyday miracles God is already doing in our lives.

It has been my experience many times throughout my life, that as soon as I say "never" about a certain circumstance or event, I do it.

A good example from the Bible is when Peter told Jesus that he loved him so much that he could never deny him. Then, very soon, he denied him not once but three times in a short period of time. Luke 22:33–34 states, "And he said unto him, Lord, I am ready to go with thee, both into prison, and to death. And he said, I tell thee, Peter, the cock shall not crow this day before that thou shalt thrice deny that thou knowest me" (KJV). In this chapter, verse 57, Peter denied Jesus for the first time, again in verse 58, and the third time in verse 60. Even though Peter denied Christ, he wept and repented. Even in this horrible situation, God taught Peter a lesson. Never say "never." You cannot always know what you will do in any given situation.

An example of that happening in my life is that because of my past work with children's church and leadership in the church, I decided I would never work in the church again. I was never going to put my heart and efforts into those things again. Well, guess what? I just recently committed to work with the children for a Christmas program.

No, this has nothing to do with Murphy's Law or the law of averages. It has to do with God knowing better than we do what he has planned for our lives. I feel that God allows me to be stretched during this process, and it becomes a learning experience that will be applied to my life. I should learn to keep my mind and heart open and my mouth closed; to listen to what God is trying to show me or tell me. It seems that I am so busy talking that I am not listening to what my heavenly Father is telling me.

Sometimes we use the word *never* when speaking about someone else's habits or a negative part of their personality that we do not appreciate or like. We *never* want to be like them, for example. This is not God's plan for us, and it could be a good lesson for us. Sometimes God allows us to be put into a position where we may not have a choice but to do something similar to what that person is doing in order to curb our judgmental attitudes.

If we ever think we are better than someone else because of sin in their lives—that we would *never* stoop to doing whatever it is that we disapprove in their lives-—we should be very careful; it's likely that we may fall into a trap. Our judgmental thinking could cause us to be put into a place where we would stoop to doing exactly what they are doing.

I have been there, done that, as the youth say. As a matter of fact, I have read that many times, those things we disapprove of in others are the very things we are dealing with in our own lives that we do not like.

That can cause us to verbalize negative statements and project them onto someone else when we see that same behavior acted out in their lives as well. It is much more important that we are aligned with God and what he thinks about us and others—that we allow God's non-critical love to direct our lives. If we will allow God to direct our words, hearts, bodies, and minds and our souls are lined up with God's Word, then we will be following God's will for our lives. He wants us, above all else, to love one another with his love, and in order to do that, the judging of one another has to go; it does not have a place in love.

We have several family members who top our prayer list every day; not one of them enjoys hearing us talk about what God has done in our lives. That's all right; we continue to pray for them. We know that at some point in God's timing their "never" may be changed into "right now." God can do anything, so we try to never say "never" when we get discouraged that they are not walking with God yet—the operative word being *yet*.

At one time in my life, a prophet gave me a prophecy that I would be like a "love-spout," spouting about God's love to others. At that time I thought that *never* in a million year could I ever do that. I thought I could *never* tell people about God's love in a way that they would be able to understand what I wanted to express to them about the love of God. I sincerely believed that nobody would be interested in my simple life stories and experiences, but here I am sharing with you the simple stories of my life, expressing God's love to you, and demonstrating my life as an example of just a few of the ways that God loves you.

Saying something can *never* be changed puts limits on God. How does that affect our faith? It puts it in a box, limiting what we believe God is able to do in our situations. If God is capable of creating human life, plant life, the birds and fowl, the heavens and the earth, can you think of anything he is not able to do? I can't. God is bigger than our situations; God is bigger than anything troubling you right now.

Never is a long time. The word *never* is infinite. Since God is the only one who knows about time, we do not have a clue. God knows, and the one thing we need to remember is that God wins. Jesus has already paid the price for your life and my life—for anyone who will accept Jesus Christ, live for him, invite him into their lives, and believe in him.

During his messages lately, our pastor has spoken about vision. He has emphasized how visionaries are sometimes the people who see things way into the future and how much faith that can require because someone who is not a visionary will only see the here and now, or the present. The visionary will see how things ultimately end up down the road, the future. A visionary lives in the future as if it is here right now. Isn't that what faith is—something we believe in that isn't yet here?

Sometimes we all should become visionaries. We should see the future and have the faith to live in the future as if it were here now regarding our families and loved ones, especially regarding their salvation, for which we are praying. Many of us have loved ones for whom we pray continually that they will accept Christ into their lives and live for him. We need to be able to know in our "knower" that God wins. It's already done. Just because we cannot see it yet doesn't mean it isn't already accomplished.

We have a lot to be thankful for; don't you agree? It may require some effort on our parts sometimes—some studying our Bibles, some prayer, some praise and worship, some stretching our faith at times, and some giving up ourselves to a God who is bigger than our circumstances. It is just so much easier when we can have someone else do everything for us, but we must be active participants in our Christian walk. It would be easier to have someone to blame for those times when things are not going our way; there's always God to blame, right?

Let me share with you what I mean. Recently, one of my family members came to me complaining of all the things that were going wrong in his life. At that time, he was right. There was a lot happening in his life that seemed to be horrible. He was dealing with it by blaming God and being angry with everyone at all times. He was not filtering these feelings through God and allowing God to lead him. Instead of taking his problems to God and asking for help, he was complaining and cursing and feeling that God did not love him anymore. Who can say they haven't felt like that at times? Be honest.

It was my job to inform him that God is not a liar. God still loves him, regardless of what happens in his life. I had to remind him that God wants to share in all of his life—

the good and the bad. Everything that was happening could be taken to God, and he could ask God to help him find the answers he desperately needed. After a few weeks, he decided to rededicate his life to God and began to take some responsibility for his own actions and decisions of the past. Now he is considering some major life changes. Hopefully, he now understands that God loves him no matter what he chooses to do in his life and that his relationship with God is more important than anything in his life. He could sit in church for weeks on end, and if his heart was not reconciled to God, nothing in his life would change.

Faith requires a one-on-one relationship with God, which brings about change in us. That means we cannot apply the word *never* to God's reigning in our lives. This family member was surprised when I told him I didn't care if he ever attended church again, as long as his heart was right with God.

I have to have faith in God that the Holy Spirit will guide this family member. His heart is what is important here. The situations in his life could be happening as reminders that God is still in control and wants to have a relationship with him. Regardless of what anyone else thinks, it is his heart's condition that is important. It is only in good shape when it is reconciled with God. Never say "never." God does know what is in our hearts, and he does care about us, every small detail included.

Story of the Dandelion

Have you ever prayed and wondered if anyone up there was listening? I'd like to share a story I received in an e-mail in mid 2009 that I found fascinating. This old man told this story about a dandelion:

> When I'd reached the point where I was wondering not if anyone was listening but if anyone was even up there at all, in the midst of this funk, feeling so completely drained, I came out of the building where I worked at the time, turned a corner, and saw this field of dandelions. There were a zillion of them—bright, yellow faces, laughing in the sunlight. Immediately, I though how like Christians they were. Everything on a dandelion can be eaten, and they are rich in Vitamin A. They even unite the old and the young—old Italian men making dandelion wine and young children send-

ing these magical parachutes through the wind—
sort of like the alpha and the omega. So here were
these little guys, ready to feed the world, and what
does the world do? In the quest for the perfect
lawn, we mow them down, gouge them out, and
glop them with poison, yet, like the followers of
Christ, their yellow flowers keep popping up to
give glory to God.

The lesson is that while I thought my prayers
weren't being heard, the Lord was actually prepar-
ing me for this great gift. If I hadn't been emptied
of all ideas and emotionally drained when I came
around that corner, all I would have seen was a
field of flowers, trees, and sky. Instead, I saw the
face of God. After that, I could no longer deny
God's calling on my life. That gift is still with me.
Whenever I see a yellow face of puffy seedpod of
the dandelion, I recognize it as a whisper of his
love for me, and I know I am not alone.

I don't know about you, but I can relate to this story. Very
recently, I felt that God not only wasn't hearing me but
had decided to take a permanent vacation away from this
particular child of his. In the first four years of our marriage, my husband and I endured many financial struggles.
We joined a wonderful church, and we prayed about tithing and agreed to commit to paying our tithes. At that
moment in time, we began to experience even more financial stress than I can relate to you. Some of the stress came
from some outrageous bills incurred in both our previous
marriages, which we both ended up having to pay; our
seven children through the blended family, my three and

his four who, even though they were all adults, required help in one form or another; and then the topper—we received a huge bill from the IRS.

This was unexpected, and the next unexpected event was my husband losing his job and being out of work for thirteen months. This was definitely not the best of times. What an understatement! What it became was a constant struggle to get the finances to even pay the bills—we're talking basic, minimum car payment, utilities, food—no extras. And, as you can guess, some of our other bills—those that were absolutely not necessities—got a bit behind, which is another understatement.

Finally, my husband went back to work, and we were able to resolve our huge IRS bill and start catching up on those other bills when suddenly, *Boom!*—guess what happened? We got another unexpected IRS bill, almost as high as the first one. There had been some kind of mix-up with the paperwork, and believe me, the IRS really socks it to you with interest. At that same time, two of our children were in dire need of transportation, and then my car broke down. My vehicle required some major repairs and had to go back to the car repair shop four times in a two-week period—to the tune of a humongous bill. Surprise. Surprise.

To be honest with you, I was beginning to question the worth of even trying to live a Christian life and pay our tithes if the reward was going to be constant financial struggle. Please understand that I was raised in a Christian home where it was just standard accounting practice to pay tithes. As far back as I can remember, my parents always paid tithes, so I knew the importance of tithing and offerings; yet I still questioned it at that time.

There is a good ending to this part of our lives, though, and that is we got through that time victoriously. How? Faith in God that he heard our prayers; he did answer our prayers. We prayed for God to give us a way out. We were blessed with an understanding IRS agent who made arrangements for monthly payments for us. Within a few months, we received a family inheritance and were able to pay the entire bill. Prior to this relief, we began to think the financial stress would never be alleviated. Never say "never." God is still in control, and he does answer our prayers. Both of the children who were in need of dependable transportation have nice vehicles at this time, and both are working fulltime jobs and doing just fine. God wins, and we need to be sure that he receives all the praise and glory for his answered prayers. He's there all the time and he uses different situations and circumstances to remind us of his care for us and his control in the daily situations or circumstances of our lives. Let me also tell you that during this time of financial struggle, we were faithful to continue paying our tithes regardless of the bills. God was so faithful to us. We never once had a utility cut off, and we never went without food. We never ran out of gas for our vehicles, and we always had plenty of everything that we needed. God is good, and he is faithful to us, and he deserves all the praise. He continues to help us in our finances and he continues to meet all of our needs.

That's not to say that it was always easy for us. There were a few times when it got down to the wire—which bill to put off until the next payday. We pared down our vehicle use to one vehicle because we lived in the country. Gasoline was on the rise, and we could not afford to take two vehicles to town every day. I confess that I started to feel anger for my heavenly Father. After all, how could he let this continue for as long as it did? It was thirteen months this time, and it had happened a few years prior for six months. At this time, I was the only one in the house working, and we had two of my children living with us.

I felt rebellious, which we all know stems from anger. I started to feel that God had totally forgotten my family and me whenever he said that he would supply all of our needs according to his riches in glory (Philippians 4:19). One operative thing to remember: sometimes what we think of as needs are wants. I struggled with some doubt about whether or not I could even trust God with our needs because he was not meeting them in the way that I expected him to—within my time frame.

Satan loves to get us to doubt God. I began to think that God had gone bankrupt, or maybe it was just my account with him that had gone bankrupt or overdrawn. We had so many problems that we had to bring to him; maybe he was tired of dealing with me.

During this time, I spoke to a mentor. This friend proceeded to tell me that God was not mad at me and that he was not tired of dealing with me—that he truly loved my family and me. She told me that God was not ignoring my prayers for help, and he was not going to neglect this child of his. She reminded me of his faithfulness to us and that he would never leave me or forsake me, meaning that he was not going to leave me to twist in the wind all alone. And, most importantly, she reminded me that I should be thankful for all that God had given me and all that he had already accomplished in my life and for the other members of my family. Basically, she told me to stop dwelling on all the bad that had happened and focus on all the good in my life. It was such great, sound advice, and I recommend you take it and run with it.

One scripture she brought to mind was that of Philippians 4:8, which admonishes us to dwell on the good things. ("Finally, brethren, whatsoever things are true, whatsoever things are honest, whatsoever things are just, whatsoever things are pure, whatsoever things are lovely, whatsoever things are of good report; if there be any virtue, and if there be any praise, think on these things.") Prior to this, I had always attempted to maintain a balance of positive thinking and faith. From a young age, I discovered that regardless of whether it actually affected my circumstances, I always felt better when I was in a thankful spirit and tried to always be thankful for even the small details in my life. Most of the time, I had been able to keep it up; however, at this time, I was absolutely drained—physically, emotionally, and spiritually. I had allowed Satan to steal my joy in serving God.

The mentor I consulted with spoke truth to me in a loving, thoughtful manner, even though I was not feeling receptive at the moment. She had been consulting God and listening to him, so she was able to hear what God was telling her to tell me. She was obedient and trusted God that I would accept the truth when I heard it. God used her to water the seed of joy that had been planted long ago in my life.

Hope is the beginning of joy, and she rekindled that hope within my heart by sharing the words God had told her. Thank God for good friends and mentors who are willing to speak God's Word to us when we need it.

The following weekend, I attended church as usual, still with some protest in my heart—some rebellion still smoldering there. I actually remember thinking, *I don't even want to be here. I don't feel loved by God right now, and I'm not sure I believe that God loves me or cares about my life.* I was actually angry with God and told him so and certainly did not feel like being thankful or praising him. I forgot who it was all about. It's not about me; it's all about him. Who was I to think I didn't need to give God praise and worship if for no other reason than the fact that he is the Great I AM.

That little seed that my friend watered had started to grow. I began to be uncomfortable during that service, and I admit, I cried during the entire service. Crying was what I needed to water that seed even more, and it grew a bit more until I began to feel hope again. I asked my Father God to forgive me for being so self-centered. Guess what? I know that he forgave me. The lesson that our pastor gave us that Sunday morning was then able to take hold, and it just happened to be one that I needed to hear about God's love for us. God used it to heal my heart. He wiped out the anger and replaced it with his joy and his peace. As the service progressed, I noticed that it was no longer some great sacrifice to give thanks and praise to God. It began to flow from my heart as my heart filled up with God's joy. God can and will do that for you too. He is not a respecter of persons. He loves *you* that much too.

If you get anything at all out of this story, I want for you to get this: You are not alone, God does love you, and God does answer prayer. God will answer your prayers too. Be aware that sometimes our timelines and the times in which God fulfills those requests are not always at the same time.

You have probably heard the expression "Stop and smell the roses." Well, I acquired a small card recently—I can't remember from where—that states, "Take the time to smell the roses and to adore their Creator." I put this on my screen saver on my computer monitor at work. It helps me to have it within view; it is a great reminder that God is an integral part of my daily life whether at work or wherever I am during the day or night. This nudges me toward an attitude of praise and worship throughout the day. It is possible to keep an attitude of praise in your mind while being involved in sundry activities throughout the day. It is great to have a specific study time each day, but I believe this should not be the only time we allow ourselves to worship God.

When I heard the story about the field of dandelions and the man's reactions to it—the way he was able to see God's face each time he viewed a dandelion and the way it acted as a reminder to him to give thanks to God—I thought this was so similar to the way that I feel about roses. I am an avid fan of roses. I feel that same way—that I am not alone when I view roses. They are so beautiful and have a wonderful aroma and such individuality in each one. There are so many fabulous flowers—and people—that God has placed in our lives for our enjoyment. Now would be a great time to meditate on those beautiful flowers (people) that God has placed in our lives. Believe me, they did not just happen to be in your life; each person in your life has a purpose in your life. I know that everyone can think of one or more wonderful people in their lives who they know are placements of God; those people bless their lives in specific ways.

We are not alone in serving God. Each one of us has so much to be thankful for. I am especially thankful for salvation—mine and that of all my family members, some of which will be happening in the near future through faith—and for my dear, loving husband with whom God bonded me. I am thankful for my Christian parents, who never cease to amaze me. I am also thankful for all the children in our family, their mates, and the beautiful grandchildren they have produced.

There is so much to be thankful for that my tiny, finite mind cannot comprehend the immensity of it all and gets boggled trying to at times. I would like to suggest to everyone that they consider all the good things in their lives; take a good look at them. Make a list of the great blessings in your life, and you may be surprised. My list never seems to end; it grows and grows.

Think about the good things when you feel bogged down with the stress and cares of your daily life. It happens to all of us. Be thankful and keep a positive attitude. Remember that God is there for you all the time. You are not alone in this journey, and God does sincerely love you so very much.

Never believe that your circumstances are here to stay. Never think you cannot change things in your life. Never say never over your life. Remember, God loves you so much that he sent his son to die on the cross just for you, and he will answer your prayers. I pray that the specific examples shared with you in this chapter will help you to see that the negative circumstances that happen in everyone's lives do not have to be forever.

Made

We are all made in the image of God. What does it mean to be made in the image of God? It means that if we give our lives over to God and allow him to reign in our hearts and souls as well as our bodies and we give him full control of our lives, we will begin to look like him. Wow! What exactly is it like to look like God? I do not believe that it is presumptuous to believe that we can look like God.

Some questions you might consider when thinking about being made in the image of God are:

1. What is your greatest asset?

2. Who are you?

3. What are your gifts?

What are the assets of God? I believe that they would be the same assets that we receive as benefits of having the Holy Spirit in our lives and living for God—allowing the Holy Spirit to lead us, which I have heard referred to as the fruits of the Spirit as listed in Galatians 5:22–23

Love	Joy
Peace	Gentleness
Goodness	Faith
Meekness	Temperance
Longsuffering	

What does it mean to be "made?" Well, "made" means to me that we are handcrafted, individually created by the hands of the Father. Wow! It's like the verse referring to God as the potter and us as the clay. The potter (God) molds our lives out of the clay into his wonderful life filled with many blessings for which we should be grateful. There is a scripture found in Romans 9:20–21 that says, "But who are you, a mere human being, to talk back to God? Shall what is formed say to the one who formed it, 'Why did you make me like this?' Does not the potter have the right to make out of the same lump of clay some pottery for noble purposes and some for disposal of refuse" (TNIV)? Our pastor stated it like this during one of his sermons: "Who are you, O man, to talk back to God? The potter has the right to make out of the same lump of clay something noble and something for common use. Do not question why God made you like you are."

That's pretty powerful for me. Who are we humans to

question God and ask, "Why me? Why did you make me the way you did? Why am I not a princess? Why do I have a dreary job that pays so little when someone else has a job to dream about? Why is my life the way it is when someone else can afford anything they want? Why? Why? Why?"

We are being admonished to enjoy our lives the way God made them. God had a purpose for our lives, and it is not unimportant. Even if your life seems dull and boring to you, if you never accomplish some huge feat in your lifetime, your life is still of major importance to God. Your obedience to him is so much more important than some huge sacrifice on your part to impress him. Like I used to often say to my children, "It ain't happening."

I have been guilty of questioning God about his reasons for certain events in my life and circumstances that I did not understand—why I had to go through certain trials, why he allowed me to gain so much weight and get gray hair. Do you know what I'm saying? Well, when I recently reread this verse in Romans 9:20–21, it jumped out at me; I felt like something had grabbed my face and made me look at it in the face. It's so real.

God made some things noble—well off, a little bit fancy—and some things for common use—us everyday, ordinary people—out of the same lump of clay. We each have a purpose, and God created us the way we are to complete his purpose of his will for our lives. We should not waste time nitpicking our lives to pieces and complaining about the way God made us. We need to concentrate on the fact that God made us for a purpose. God has given each of us different talents, gifts, abilities, and circumstances.

Nobody can attain our goals or our purposes for us, and nobody else has the ability to accomplish that specific purpose; only you and only I can do what God has purposed for us to do.

We should all do whatever God has given us to do to the best of our abilities and do it as unto God. If God has only given you one talent, and you use that talent for him, it will grow into more and you will be rewarded with much more as a result of faithfully using your talent for God's purposes. God made some of us to be day laborers, some to be secretaries, some to be homemakers, librarians, bankers, stockbrokers, car salesmen, mechanics, some waitresses, dishwashers, cooks, janitors, artists, pastors, musicians, salesclerks, policemen, CEOs of major corporations, the list goes on and on.

My point in naming some ordinary jobs is that God made us, and he has purposed his will to come forth through our lives, regardless of what our social or economic positions are. Whatever job you have, know that you are blessed in that job and that promotion comes from God. Your faithfulness will attract God's attention, and God is the promoter. If we are faithful with the one talent, exercise it, improve on it, like the parable of the Ten Minas found in Luke 19:11–26, where a master brought several servants before him prior to leaving town on a trip and gave them money to take care of his home and lands while he was gone. When he called them to report on what they had done, one had gained ten more minas, the second gained five more, and the last one had hidden his in the ground and not done anything with it! We don't want to be that third servant.

God is the Creator who made you what you are. You should appreciate the gifts and abilities God placed within you that make you unique and special. Enjoy the fact that God made you who you are and what you are, whether you intend to remain in the place you are currently at or intend to be promoted. You are blessed to be in the job you have now. You are blessed to be living in a wonderful country where you have the right to choose your profession and where you want to live.

How do we get made by God and receive true blessings rather than the kind of counterfeit blessing that Jacob received because he was not prepared to wait for the real thing? Jacob was the younger brother of Esau. The older brother traditionally received a blessing from his father passing on his inheritance to the oldest son. Jacob, with the help of his mother, Rachel, tricked their father, Isaac, into giving the blessing for the older son to him. Listed below are some ways to become a recipient of the true blessings of God:

1. Walk in someone else's shoes

2. Talk blessings. Renew your mind.

3. Practice. If you want to walk on water, you must step out of the boat.

4. Exercise your faith.

5. Change your image; adopt the nature of Christ.

If we would be willing to practice these things, we would see that the transformation has been accomplished. It is complete. We will be made in the image of Christ.

Do you know who you are? Are you made? Do you know if you are made? You are made in the image of God; you look like him. Refer to the verses below:

> Then God said, "Let us make man in our image, in our likeness and let them rule over the fish of the sea and the birds of the air, over the livestock, over all the earth, and over all the creatures that move along the ground."
>
> Genesis 1:26

> So God created man in his own image, in the image of God he created him, male and female he created them.
>
> Genesis 2:1

We are created to take dominion, or authority, over our own families, finances, health, homes, cars, music, TVs, free time, jobs—everything in our lives. We have the power through the Holy Spirit. We cannot do it alone, but through the power of the Holy Spirit, we can do all things through Christ Jesus who strengthens us (Philippians 4:13). Sometimes we just have to be willing to reach out and grab the reins back from Satan and allow God to reign in our lives.

If you have been praying for something or someone for a long time and have not received your answer, don't give up. Your answer is on the way. Remember, our timing and God's are not always the same. You are made in the image of God through the blood of Jesus. You can expect an answer from your Father. Jesus had absolutely no doubt that when he prayed to the Father that God was going to answer his prayers. We should have the same confidence in our prayers with our same heavenly Father. If you have said yes to God and have accepted him into your heart and life, you are made, and you can expect God to do the same for you that he does for any and all of his other children, including miracles.

What image do you present to others? How can you change your city or your community if your image is negative? What Jesus are you representing? What do you have that someone else might need? It is our job to establish God's kingdom on this earth; we are to take dominion over our families and over everything in our lives in order to see that kingdom established. Jeremiah 1:5 says that we were designed before we were born. The future has already happened. We are already made. Are you walking in that?

The plans are already here. It's like a blueprint that you and I probably would have a difficult time deciphering; an architect could glance at it and be able to tell us exactly what every little line or broken line meant and how large a building would be by how many inches the lines are. He would see where every faucet or door would go or anything else you may want to know about the building. He knows how to read blueprints.

There is a plan for our lives also, and even though we may not be able to see the overall picture and read those blueprints for our lives, God knows exactly what each thing on our blueprint means in the overall plan of our lives. Jeremiah 29:11 reads, "For I know the plans I have for you,' declares the Lord, 'plans to prosper you and not to harm you, plans to give you hope and a future'" (TNIV).

After reading that verse, maybe we should ask our Father God, the architect of our lives, "What is your blueprint, or will, for my life? What do you want me to do? What is your will for me to accomplish in my life? Which path did you choose for me to follow?"

God knows the plan, and he is the only one who knows the plan—the great architect who can read the plans and knows exactly what they say about our lives.

No mistake is beyond repair. Did we build our house without consulting the great architect's plan—without asking our Father what his plans were for our lives? It's not the end. Do not accept it as the end. That house can be torn down and rebuilt by the great architect according to his blueprint for our lives, and, if need be, he can tear that house down and keep rebuilding it for us until it suits his plan and fits his will for us. There is no limit to the building that the master architect can do. God has had this plan from the beginning of time.

Jacob manipulated his birthright, as we are told in the book of Genesis in the Bible. He did not wait for the true blessing to come to him. Jacob had received a prophecy about his inheritance, or birthright, and like so many of us, he couldn't wait and took matters into his own hands. Just a side note: Jacob was listening to someone else instead of listening to God; he conspired with his mother to get his inheritance. It is highly likely that if you and I are listening to someone else other than God that this other person may have his or her own agenda and not necessarily our best interests at heart. Sometimes it may seem as if this person has your best interests in mind, as in the case of Jacob, but don't count on it.

Before you make a move on what someone else tells you, check with God; as I always say, filter it through God's judgment first. You may find that God has different plans for you than you had considered. In Genesis 27:19, Jacob fooled his dad by lying to and deceiving him. He received the counterfeit blessing rather than waiting for the true blessing, but he was already blessed and didn't need to take matters into his own hands to steal his brother's birthright. It had already been prophesied that Jacob would receive his birthright.

As we find in the thirty-second chapter of Genesis, Jacob had to leave his homeland and wander around for years. He even had to hide from his brother Esau. In the twenty-fourth verse of this chapter, Jacob sent every member of his family away and was alone and wrestled with a "man" all night. We find in the next verse that when the "man" realized that Jacob was not giving up, he touched Jacob's thigh and it was out of joint. Jacob asked him for a blessing, and his name was changed. Verse 28 says, the "man" who wrestled with Jacob said, "Thy name shall be called no more Jacob, but Israel; for as a prince has thou power with God and with man and has prevailed." After that, Jacob renamed the place that he had received his blessing and stated that he had seen God face-to-face and his life had been preserved. This was Jacob's true blessing. Like Jacob, we do not want the counterfeit blessing, but the real thing. What we need is to wait on the true blessing and not try to make it happen on our own, as Jacob did. Waiting is not as easy as it sounds. Waiting for the true blessing requires more patience than some of us have, and it also necessitates being alone with God, like Jacob was when he wrestled with the "man." It also means that we can't always choose the path of least resistance; rather, we must be willing to go where God is telling us to go. Jacob struggled and overcame, and he became the one called "Israel." Sometimes we have to fight or press through until God's blessings come; persevere and do not give up on that promised blessing.

No matter where you are in life, you can have a new start. Start over; you can still make an impact in your life. I have noticed a mellowing in some Christians when they gain wisdom in their later years in life, and God can truly use that to mentor the younger men and women within the church body. Do not think that you have arrived at a point in your life when God can no longer use you. He can and he will if you will allow him. Don't settle for the counterfeit.

Take dominion, or authority, over your life. Step out of the boat. Exercise your faith. You can make an impact on your family, your home, your neighborhood, your city, your state, your country and your world. Walk through the open doors that God has provided for you, and don't give up, but take dominion. It is done. You have authority in your life. You have been made for a purpose—to serve God using those abilities, gifts, talents, and all that God has given you.

Because of my past mistakes, I felt there was no way I

could be made into God's image. I knew God in my youth, walked away from God, and became involved in partying and drinking. I decided I could never be good enough for God to work through me. My life was a mess, with divorce and many bad choices. At that time, I believed that God didn't have any use for my life, even though I had rededicated my life to him. Through the years, God has used me to counsel with single moms and others who have been through similar circumstances. Never say "never." If God can use my life full of mistakes to help someone else, he can use you.

Under the
Circumstances

"Under the circumstances"—have you considered that phrase before? Pondered it? Thought it through? People are always saying "under the circumstances," and usually they use it with a negative twist. Stop and think: when was the last time someone used that phrase in a conversation with you? Usually it is used to indicate that a change of plans took place in regard to the current circumstances. Instead of participating in something you planned to do, "under the circumstances," you chose to do something else.

Choose your circumstances. Maybe you can't choose everything that happens in your life; however, you can choose to get through the circumstances instead of being beneath the circumstances—under the circumstances. I can choose to walk in victory rather than let the circumstances get me down.

Walking in victory may seem like a dream that is unattainable, but it can be as simple and as easy as deciding to do something and then doing it. "Just do it"—Nike's famous slogan—can be applied here. It can be that easy for us if we choose to let it be. How? By vocalizing our faith. Yes—saying it out loud then practicing that faith. Appropriate what Jesus has done for us. How? Through thankfulness. Whenever you think that the circumstances are more than you can bear, when they get as heavy as a sack of rocks on your back, just remember to thank God for those good things in your life. Begin to dwell on the good.

If you can take a baby step of faith by beginning to be thankful for just one little thing, you will find it easier the next time to add another item and another, and soon you will find a lot to be thankful for. Many times when I first begin praying, I am speechless—can't think of one single word to say, so I fall back on my tried and true standby, the Lord's Prayer. It has all the elements of prayer that we need, and it was given to us as an example for prayer:

> Our Father, who art in heaven, hallowed be thy name.
>
> Thy kingdom come, thy will be done, on Earth as it is in heaven.
>
> Give us this day our daily bread, and forgive us our trespasses as
>
> We forgive those who have trespassed against us,

And lead us not into temptation, but deliver
us from evil,
For thine is the kingdom, and the power, and
the glory forever.
Amen

Matthew 6:9–13

Choose life every day by choosing to be thankful for the
life God gave to you. Everyone has things in their lives
for which it is difficult to be thankful. I am not saying you
must be thankful for abuse if you live with it, but begin
to be thankful for God's protection of you up to this time,
if you are able. If you aren't at a point that you can be
thankful for that, you should be able to find something in
your life to be thankful for. It could be God's love, Jesus
dying on the cross for you, a good friend who loves you
and accepts you totally, or resources that God has placed
in your life, for example.

Many people have difficult circumstances in their lives,
and I cannot imagine how they get through those circumstances. I have lived through physical, sexual, verbal, and
emotional abuse myself, and God has allowed me to come
out of all of it; I am so very thankful for that. I have learned
to be thankful in different situations, even though I have
been known to complain at times—even now. There is
always something to be thankful for. You may have to
dig deeper sometimes; however, there will be those other
times that you don't have to look far to be thankful. The
important point here is that you thank God for whatever
good there is in your life. It could be something as simple

as a flower outside your window, or it could be your children, a home, a vehicle, a friend, your church, or your pastor. You get the idea. I keep a list in my purse almost all the time, and it goes from one purse to another—I'm famous for changing purses often—and that list is my uplifting list of things for which to thank God. Thankfulness puts us over the circumstances instead of being trod on under the circumstances. Soon, once you begin to be thankful, it grows like a smile grows—from one face to another to a whole crowd—into praise and then to worship, and it is very powerful. It is also empowering. Who doesn't want to experience that empowerment?

There's a scripture found in 2 Corinthians 5:21 that says, "For he made him who knew no sin to be sin for us, that we might become the righteousness of God in him." You and I are the righteousness of God through Christ. Because Jesus gave himself on the cross for us, now we can become the righteousness of God through Jesus Christ.

That scripture has helped me many times and has become almost like a mantra for me when I feel ungodly, unloved, or ugly. Everyone has times when they feel that way; however it sure doesn't help when someone is telling you how awful you are or how ugly you are daily. I've been there, and I don't ever want to go there again. With my faith in God, I don't have to go there unless I choose to go.

There are days it would be easy to fall into that trap. If you will begin to say a few words of thanks to the heavenly Father and then be still for a while and listen, he will respond to you. You need never feel lonely, ugly, lost, or hurt again because by the stripes of Jesus, you can overcome and be healed, if you will ask. Ask for it, and then be thankful for it. Give thanks with a grateful heart. Give thanks unto the one who died for you.

Walking in victory is not something you can never accomplish. It is simply living in victory one day—one hour, one minute at a time. What is living in victory? It is speaking out the faith that you have within your heart and letting your faith be declared through your mouth. It is letting what you expect from God be known to people in your life and knowing that God will fulfill his Word. That doesn't mean you can ask for selfish things and expect to receive them all the time. When you pray according to the will of God, asking for those things that are necessary for your life so that you can fulfill God's will in and through your life, you can expect God to answer those prayers for you. Sometimes God will answer our selfish, self-centered prayers—usually to teach us a lesson—but I feel that most of the time, our selfish prayers, which do not take into consideration God's will for our lives, don't accomplish anything but wasting our time and God's.

God does not change; circumstances do. Please don't live under the circumstances anymore. Allow God's light and his love to shine through you by allowing the faith in your heart to come out. As it has been said in the Bible in various ways, what you have in your heart will come out of your mouth. Whatever is dearest to your heart will come out, and you will talk about it. If God is the dearest thing to you and he is the center of your life, then he is going to be the main topic, so let it out.

Set yourself up for victory by the words you speak

daily. Build your faith by reading God's Word, and you will begin to grow his seed in your heart while at the same time gaining wisdom. Soon, it will come out of your mouth. You are the righteousness of God in Christ. Jesus is your truth, your wisdom, your righteousness, and your life, and through your faith, you can become the righteousness of God through Christ by accepting Jesus into your heart and allowing your mouth to declare his goodness and testify to his love.

By testifying to God's love, you will be choosing life every day. You can begin to get on top of those circumstances in your life that may not be so pleasing to you. Give them to God, and leave them in his care. He knows better than us what needs to be handled, and he's so much better than us at handling everything if we will just allow him to do so. Who better?

Set your heart, your love, on Jesus. Make him your habitat and your dwelling place—that place where you abide, that place where you stay. You can begin to experience that by continually being in a place of prayer, even throughout the mundane things you must do every day. I was a bookkeeper for a car dealership until 2005, and I found it was a great time to pray for my church family members during my editing time when I did the same chores every morning. It is possible to stay in an attitude of constant prayer by quoting God's Word in your own mind. This will help you in ways by which you may be surprised later; for example, when you are in need of a particular scripture and it comes to mind. I can testify to that with a case from some time ago.

My friend needed to hear a word, and God brought that exact scripture that she needed to hear to my mind, and I was able to share it with her. I had forgotten that I even knew that verse.

Sometimes I had to get out of my office and go the ladies' room to get a few minutes of quiet so that I could be alone with God a short time and just pray to stay on top of the circumstances. It was always beneficial to both me and my office mates. Just those few minutes spent alone with God equipped me and enabled me to use those opportunities to witness for him whenever the opportunity arose. Hopefully, I wouldn't have to apologize for something said wrong or in anger because of those few minutes of respite away from the bustle, noise, and stress of the office.

Circumstances occurred often in my office about which I was not pleased or that I found offensive. Sometimes I found it very difficult to keep my mouth closed, and sometimes I failed in that area. During those times when it was more difficult to contain my mouth, I tried to get away and take an alone-with-God break so that I could develop a better attitude and become a more positive witness. I find this method of getting away with God even for a few moments in times of stress is also helpful in my life issues today. However, I am still under construction. Aren't we all?

God has always dealt with me very gently and lovingly at those times. He teaches me how to keep from always having to state my opinion. One thing I am learning is that even if I am right, it can cause more damage than necessary to always have to express my knowledge or opinion. It's not always best to be right if you have to blurt it out all the time. My husband hates it when I am right about certain topics, but I have been gifted with discernment. Sometimes it really irks people. I have found that many times, those of us who possess the gift of discernment don't always practice the gift of tact. We also have to be wise about how we present these gifts that God has given to us, even when we think we know the right answers.

Sometimes I have to ask God to help me forgive someone for something—whether they know they need to be forgiven or not and whether I consider it major or minor—so that the peace of God can be restored to my soul and so that I can become a more positive influence or witness in the lives of the people I meet every day. We have children and grandchildren in and out of our home every day who all need to see God's love shine forth out of me, and I want it to come straight out of my mouth via my heart.

The circumstances are not winning, even though Satan would love to see that happen. Satan hates to lose, and he will fight dirty to win. God wins. In the end, we need to remember that God wins, and he can win right now if we will allow him to in our lives—if we focus on not letting the circumstances dictate our lives and allowing God to reign in our hearts, souls and lives. Have you heard the song, "Oh How He Loves You and Me" (words and music written by Kurt Kaiser)? It is an old hymn we sang in the Pentecostal church I attended throughout my youth. Isn't that great? We can all be victorious and live on top of the mountain, on top of the circumstances. Thank you, Father God.

Priorities, Priorities, Priorities

"Priorities"
By Heather Whitestone

Life is too short to
Spend it on the
Urgent while
Important things
Slide by unnoticed.

What are your priorities? Do you always get them right? I don't. I always want to but don't always seem to have the action to fit the desires. When we can stay in an attitude of prayer throughout the day and any time we are awake, it is much easier to stick to our priorities and follow them through.

From my experiences with others, as well as myself, I find that most of us have trouble setting priorities. Of course, priorities can be considered to be age appropriate for some people. However, no matter our ages or circumstances, we should all have a set of priorities for our lives, and God should be priority number one.

I learned how to set priorities after I had experienced partying and drinking for a while and realized that was not a lifestyle I wanted to see my children become involved in. I am grateful they were young enough not to remember a lot about my partying days. I am blessed to be able to say that after making the decision to put God as top priority in my life, all three of them have come to have a personal relationship with God. Here is another instance I can emphasize never say "never." I just knew I had messed up so badly and was fearful that my children would not come to God as a result of my prior bad choices, but God is good.

A priority is a personal decision we make, either consciously or unconsciously, whereby we place our focus, our time, and our love. This goes back to what's in your heart and what you love the most. What is precious to you? My family is my second priority after God.

God has placed fabulous people in my life and allowed me to join with them by becoming family members together through fellowship and growing together through praise and worship to our heavenly Father. Whatever your priorities, you know that God has to be number one—at the top of the list. Otherwise, your life, however successful it may seem, is not going to work. Wherever you place your list of to-dos for your life, or whatever your personal agenda may include, God's will for your life has to be your number-one priority.

When I worked as a personal assistant to the CEO of a large company in San Antonio, Texas, we had strategy meetings to discuss priorities for the day, the week, for a month at a time, for a year at a time, and for five to ten years down the road. At that time, we set our priorities and established goals that we expected to achieve within each time frame. Priorities were important in attaining our goals for the company, and we were all included in the decision-making process.

In the same vein, our priorities are very important in helping us to get to the heart of our lives and be able to accomplish what God has placed in our hearts to accomplish for him—his will for our lives, our purpose.

Priorities can bring success if they are placed in the proper perspective. I always say, "Don't make a promise to anyone if you aren't one hundred percent sure that you can fulfill it." Really, not one of us can be one hundred percent sure of our own capability to accomplish everything in order to be able to fulfill a promise that may have been made in haste. I do not like for people to promise me something if they have no intent or ability to accomplish it.

Don't make promises you can't keep; that's a catch-phrase my children have heard all of their lives, mostly from Mom. I wouldn't make them promises just to pacify them, especially if I did not know if the promises were possible. This is one mantra I have attempted to apply to my life. I have been associated with a very diverse group of people for years, both through my employment situations and through my church affiliations and friends outside the church. My children have always had a lot of different kinds of friends, and not one of the three I raised shared the same social circle or group of friends. Now they are all adults and live in different cities. One is a computer tech, one an artist, and another is in the military. This should tell you how diverse they are now.

I refuse to commit to making promises that will keep me from being able to fulfill my promises made to my marriage and family, including my church family. I want to allow the gifts that God has given to me to be used by God, and my first commitment is to him. My ultimate purpose is to bring as many people to Christ as possible through use of my abilities, talents, gifts, life examples, and whatever means God has given to me. This is such a high priority for me that sometimes I have been known to turn down work opportunities within the church because I believe that one person can only do so much. I feel that we must honor our first commitments and not heap so many on ourselves that we won't be able to fulfill those first commitments to the best of our abilities. It is so easy to be spread too thin.

Our most important priority of commitment should be to love God first then to love one another as Christ has loved the church. This was the final commandment we received from Jesus before he went back to heaven. The way I do this is by using the skills, talents, abilities, knowledge, discernment, prophetic gifts, music, praise, and worship to glorify God. I do whatever I can to help God's other children. Love is an action verb, not just a sit-back-and-watch kind of noun.

Many times, we feel that something is just too big for us to accomplish so we just won't commit to it at all. One good way to minimize that huge object in the way is simply to tackle it in steps; break it down. Start by making a list of priorities—small ones, at first. As you achieve one goal, enlarge it and go onto the next goal, which is bigger than the first one. Before you realize it, you have accomplished the whole project. If you have a list of priorities, you won't be as likely to be deterred or sidetracked by Satan's constant interferences and his little foxes, which are continually trying to get to your vines. He does try to sidetrack all of us by throwing whatever obstacles he can in our way. If you can't go around them, just go straight through them. Just don't stop; keep going.

Did you know that you are top priority with God? Yes—he even gave up his son for your life. Jesus gave up his life's blood and his very life for you, and then he rose again to fulfill his promises to his people. We are his chosen people. You are his favorite child, and God loves you so much that he was willing to send his own beloved son, Jesus Christ, to die on the cross for you. You are the passion of God. You are the passion of Christ. If you haven't seen the movie *The Passion of the Christ,* directed by Mel Gibson, I recommend that you do. It is so incredibly realistic and very closely depicts the day Jesus gave up his life and all his suffering on the cross, as well as the hours prior to it. It shows when he rose again, fulfilling the Old Testament prophecy.

For me, it was a powerful reminder that God cares

enough for me to send Jesus to die on the cross just for me—and Jesus died just for you. If you were the only sinner on the earth—and we have all sinned and come short of the glory of God, according to Romans 8:23—God would have sent Jesus to die on the cross just for you.

It is like the story in the Bible of the shepherd found in Matthew 18:12–14 who had one hundred sheep. One went missing, and the shepherd left the other ninety-nine to find the one that was missing. It is the same way with our heavenly Father; he loves us that much. You and I are God's first priority. Why? His love for us is number-one priority for God because he wants to have a relationship with each one of us. We are his children, whom he created. He knew each one of us before we were in our mothers' wombs. God knew every detail about us even before we were born.

Families are important. That is a truth that we all learn as we mature in age and wisdom. When we are young, much of the time, we haven't really learned how very important our families are to us. It is usually after we have experienced a few of the hard knocks of growing up in today's world that we learn to appreciate the families God has given to us. I believe families should be high on everyone's list of priorities. Everyone should have a family with whom they can share their lives. If you don't have a close biological family, then you need to make it a high priority to gather people around you as your own family unit; you can learn more about God with them. This created family should be comprised of people who will help you to seek out his will for your life, as well as have some accountability with you. In my family, when one is going through something either good or bad, we always pray for one another. We know we have the ability to call any of the other family members and ask them to help us pray for something. When one is able to help another, using personal resources, we share in the problem. That is my idea of the family God means us to have within the family of God.

I have a personal example to share with you about the importance of family. On December 8, 2008, my husband and I were on our way home from Midland, Texas, shopping for final Christmas gifts for our grandchildren who live in Indiana. It was our plan to ship them all off the following morning. My husband received a call on his cell phone and answered it. His face immediately turned white, and he pulled over to the side of the road. (This was before it was a legal no-no to talk on the phone while driving.) I turned to look at him and saw a tear starting to form in the corner of his eye and knew this was bad, really bad. Our oldest son, who lives in Indiana, had been involved in a shooting and was not expected to live throughout the night. When he got off the phone, we immediately called our life group leader and requested prayer and told them that we would be leaving in the morning for Indiana. Within a few hours, we had received several calls from friends and family offering help. Our life group leaders came over to pray with us and left handing us money to help with the trip. My nephew by marriage came over to pray with us and left, giving us money to help. My parents prayed with us on the way out of town and gave us money to help, and my sister had stopped by my parents' home that morning, knowing we were dropping by before leaving town, and left a card and money to help. We were blown away by all the love shown to us that day by our church family as well as our natural family. We received phone calls every day of that two-week journey from people saying they were praying for us and for our son. We were so overwhelmed by God's love for us shown through his people.

Just a footnote to this story, we returned home two weeks later very tired but happy our son was still alive. We received a call from another family member that this son had been saved and was asking for a Bible! Praise God, he is still in control. You never know what route you will be taking, but you can know that God will lead you to his quiet and safe place to rest when needed, as he did for us. Many times, God will use friends and family to help you get through something or to show his love.

It also helps to have accountability to another Christian or group of Christians, as I briefly mentioned in the previous paragraphs. That accountability doesn't mean that you are bound to a specific group of people, but that you can bond with those people. What it means is that you are able to more closely follow your God-given, God-approved priorities and that you have people who care about you. They will be there when you need help, and you can also help them to adhere to their set of God-given abilities. This person or group of people whom you are willing to be accountable to must be of like faith, or it won't help you.

As you gather these people into your own family unit, you will require a great deal of wisdom from God. He will unite you with family members whom he chooses. He knows whom you will love and who will love you with his love, and they will benefit your life. Ask God to bring the people into your life who can minister to your life and who will be supportive of the priorities that God has placed on your heart. All you have to do is to ask, and he will soon start sending them into your life.

My husband and I have started attending a home study, which is called a Life Group, through our church. In the months that we have been attending the group meetings in different homes, we have begun to feel very close to the people in the group and feel connected with them. We also feel accountable to them and know that whenever we need prayer, the first place we will be going for prayer help is to our Life Group members. When we have good news to share, this is also the first place we usually share it, other than with immediate family members. It is so beneficial to our lives, and sometimes when we start to get a little out of line in our lives, we also have people who will help us get back in line through our accountability with them and theirs with us.

What might be some of God's priorities? I strongly believe that God's priorities include having a close relationship with each one of his children. He's so ready to make you a priority of his, if you will just ask him. Try to remember it's all about him. He's there loving you, even when you don't know him yet or even if you may be angry with God for the things that have transpired in your life or for something that happened to you in the past. Maybe you are angry with God for something that is going on right now. He still loves you. Again, I'll remind you: God does not change. We might change, circumstances change, and the seasons change—both in the natural and supernatural—but God's love for us does not change. The following is a statement I heard on one of my favorite Christian television shows, *Touched by an Angel*. Although it's a fiction show, the angels are always pointing people to God. One of the angels quoted these words to someone they were trying to help as a part of the story.

> When God is no longer real to you and you feel you've lost your faith, go back to the place that you last saw him; he's there waiting for your return with open arms. He truly loves you more than you will ever know. God really does exist, and he really does care about you and your life. He will love you even when you don't return his love. He will still be there for you.

I know how true that statement is. When I heard it, the words pierced my heart, and I immediately went to my trusty, old computer and typed it up verbatim. I printed out several copies and placed them in strategic places around my home—plastered it all over the place. It means to me that I am a top priority with God and that he wants to have a relationship with me. Wow! What a wonderful priority to be. You are his priority too. He has made each one of us his top priority. Never think God doesn't love you or think about you and want the best for your life. This is supported by Jeremiah 29:11, which says: "For I know the thoughts I think toward you, saith the Lord, thoughts of peace, and not of evil, to give you an expected end" (KJV).

That's Just the Way It Is

I do not believe that we have to accept things like abuse and say things like, "That's just the way it is." We don't have to accept sin in our own lives because we do not feel we can do any better, and we do not have to continue to live in sin. That's *not* just the way it is, and that's *not* just the way that person is.

No—prayer can and does change things. Prayer changes people. Prayer changes circumstances. Prayer can move mountains. Prayer with faith just the size of a mustard seed can move a mountain. Faith the size of a grain of a mustard seed is discussed in Matthew 17:20: "And Jesus said unto them, Because of your unbelief; for verily I say unto you, If ye have faith as a grain of mustard seed, ye shall say unto this mountain. Remove hence to yonder place; and it shall remove; and nothing shall be impossible unto you." The disciples were complaining that their prayers were not as effective as those of Jesus. Sometimes our prayers may not be answered within our specified time frames because God created time; God is all about time. He knows the right time for things to be accomplished because he can see the overall picture that we do not see. Sometimes our agendas are not in sync with God's agenda, but he has the overall blueprint; we only see a part of the plan and think we know better than God sometimes what needs to be done and when it needs to be done. Isn't God gracious to us to even allow us to think that way sometimes? He's the great architect. We are his children. He knows what's best for us and when the best time is to answer our prayers so that his will can be fulfilled in our lives.

My family found out several years ago that prayer can change circumstances because prayer—talking with God—is effective whenever we are in a relationship with our Father. My son became involved with drugs and had moved in with a young lady who was addicted. She had a regular drug dealer who expected my son to pray for her drugs. When he refused, this dealer made threats against my son and his entire family. It seemed hopeless, and we lived in fear for several weeks, knowing each day could be our last if this dealer did not receive the money he felt was owed to him. We regrouped as a family and began to pray for answers to this serious threat. God answered our prayers by having my son go and stay with his father, who lived in another part of the state. When he moved in with his father, he began to attend church and rededicated his life to God. Never say "never," because God won that battle on our family's behalf and we no longer live in fear. Ultimately, when God answers our prayers, prayer changes peoples' lives. Prayer changes the person praying for someone else, and it changes the person for whom someone is praying. The thing that has been the most difficult for my family to learn—and believe me, we are still learning it—is that our time and God's time are very rarely the same. I am always in a hurry for things to happen because I see ahead, down the road, and I know that certain things have to happen to accomplish that thing down the road. God doesn't always have his clock set with mine. Sometimes I want the people I am praying for to just hurry up and come to God because I can see what awesome Christians they will become and I know a small part of what God has in store for them due to some prophetic word God has given to me regarding their lives. Guess what? I'm still waiting on most of them to come to God, yet, because of my faith in God, I know that he is working on them and using his wisdom to bring them in. My agenda seems to get in the way sometimes, but God is so gracious to me. He has allowed me to see some of the people I've prayed for have some miracles come about, and some came to a relationship with him.

Sometimes when we pray for others it requires some work on our part. We may have to put a lot of time and invest a lot of tears—give up ourselves to them in different areas of their lives to show them the love of God. Sometimes we just have to stand on God's promises to us. When we have done all we know to do, then we have to stand on the promises that God has given to us. This reminds me of a song we used to sing in church growing up titled "Standing on the Promises." It's a great hymn and the words could be applied here—standing on the promises of God.

I had a Christian friend once whose husband decided he wanted a divorce. During the time I was praying for her, I would ask God to give me some wise words to share with her. The only word I kept getting was to tell her that she needed "to stand." Well, I held off telling her this because I just knew that God would have some big, meaningful message for me to deliver to her-some large pronouncement that would help cure her problems. But God kept giving me the same word for her—*stand*. Finally, I wrote her a card with that message, and then, two or three days later, I called her to be sure she had received my card. When we started visiting and I apologetically told her what I had received from God, she laughed. It was exactly the same word God had given to her, and it was confirmation that she was truly hearing from God. Well, I also received confirmation that I had heard from God when sharing that information with her. Sure made me feel better too. Sometimes it's not in the large, overwhelming words we expect or in huge actions; sometimes it's just a small word of encouragement. This friend and I agreed to stand on God's word for her at that time. She came through that time beautifully. I wish I could say she and her husband were reconciled. They were not, but she is now remarried and very happy.

Sometimes the knowledge that we may need to put some work into a situation, other than prayer, keeps us from praying more diligently for someone. Change usually means there has to be some stretching and some growth, and growth is not always easy, pain-free, or comfortable. Sometimes we are required to get outside of our comfort zones, and many times that can be a scary thing. When my boys were going through major physical growth spurts, we'd laugh and say they were having growing pains. Sometimes the younger one still says he's having growing pains, and he's six-foot-two and wears a size fourteen shoe. Growing and being stretched in the spirit can be painful and uncomfortable. But it is necessary for us to be able to become who God has planned for us to become.

Our faith has to be stretched sometimes, almost to the breaking limit. There has to be room to grow. It is also our faith that renews our hope and enables us to continue to pray—to be steadfast in prayer when things don't happen as quickly as we think they should. We must be persistent; the stretching produces the changes in our lives and in the lives of the people we love and pray for. Prayer really does change things and peoples' lives. We don't have to accept that it's just the way it is or just the way they are. I have learned through my prayer experiences that God can change even the most awful circumstances. God can change peoples' hearts, which, in the end, changes peoples' lives. It does not have to be "that way."

I used to make excuses for people in my past relationships, which only served to empower them to continue in their abusive habits and actions; I said, "That's just the way he is." However God allowed me to see through another relationship experience that it does not have to be that way. God has used my family members many times to teach me life lessons, especially my children. He used them all at different times to teach me about life changes and how it does not have to be "that way."

We have had some horrible experiences through the years. Some of that time, I was a single mother, but some of the worst times were when I was married to the wrong person. During those times when I was a single mother, I had three children with me to raise part of the time. Those times when I included God in my plans, my life had much more hope and meaning. At other times, when I was rebellious and thought I could do things on my own, I found that my life did not have the joy that it did at other times. When God was in control, it took some of the burden off of me, and I was able to feel more joy. God needs to be in control of our lives.

Change is said to be the one thing you can depend on. Thank God we had some positive changes in our home. As a result of those God-induced changes, which came about through prayer and our willingness to allow God to control our home, we are a very close-knit family now.

Sometimes it is easier to accept poor behavior rather than be responsible and disciplined enough to come against the bad behavior ourselves—to correct it and pray for change. I can personally tell you that it is very rewarding when you hang in there and continue to pray for God's changes to come about. When they do, change is much easier to accept.

What if it takes too long? Again, God's timing and ours are not always the same, but he knows what he's doing. Sometimes it takes longer than we feel it should for God to bring about the necessary changes. It's good to remind yourself that God never changes and that he is faithful. He will answer those prayers that are prayed in earnest and in accordance with his will. We just need to be persistent enough and want that change enough to push into God for the answers. I believe it will happen.

God is still the same yesterday, today, and tomorrow. That means that his promises to his children don't and won't change. He is faithful and just. When Jesus was praying in the Garden of Gethsemane with his disciples, prior to being taken to die on the cross, his disciples went to sleep instead of praying as they had been asked to do. Jesus said to them, "Could you not keep watch with me for one hour" (Matthew 26:40)?

We must be diligent and remain persistent if we really do want to see those changes come about, and that means we have to keep bringing those needs to God's attention. I have a reputation in the accounting world for being like a bulldog when it comes to researching some accounting problems; I stick with it until I find the problem. It might take a while, but I finally do find it; stubbornness has its advantages, I guess. We have to have that kind of persistence until our prayers are answered. We cannot give up. What if you gave up the night before God planned to answer your prayer? Remain diligent in your prayers. If they are of importance to you, they are also of importance to God.

In a recent lesson, I heard this phrase and it really stuck with me: "The victory is won in my prayer time when I put on the whole armor of God. I can live in victory."

(Thank God.) This should give us some relief, knowing how dependable God is.

Praising God and prayer can bring about the changes that need to occur in our lives. First, they will bring about a change in us. God is always there to hear our prayers; even though Satan would have you convinced that God is not listening to you anymore or that he doesn't care enough to answer your prayers.

Previously, I stated that if we put on the whole armor of God, we can obtain the victory and walk in victory. The whole armor of God as found in Ephesians 6:11–18 is:

1. Loins girded with truth

2. Breastplate of righteousness

3. Feet shod with the preparation of the gospel of peace

4. Shield of faith

5. Helmet of salvation

6. Sword of the Spirit - the Word of God

7. Praying always in the Spirit

The King James Version of these scriptures reads:

> Put on the whole armour of God, that ye may be able to stand against the wiles of the devil. For we wrestle not against flesh and blood, but against principalities, against powers, against the rulers of the darkness of this world, against spiritual wick-

edness in high places. Wherefore take unto you the whole armour of God, that ye may be able to withstand in the evil day, and having done all, to stand. Stand therefore, having your loins girt about with truth, and having on the breastplate of righteousness; And your feet shod with the preparation of the gospel of peace; Above all, taking the shield of faith, wherewith ye shall be able to quench all the fiery darts of the wicked. And take the helmet of salvation, and the sword of the Spirit, which is the word of God: Praying always with all prayer and supplication in the Spirit, and watching thereunto with all perseverance and supplication for all saints.

Notice that all of the things cover the front, not the back. Do you realize that God's got your back? He's our "rearguard." If we can put on the whole armor or God, we will be able to pray effectively. Then we will be able to appropriate God's promises for our lives and start to see our prayers being answered. At that point, we can see the changes come about.

When we don't understand why a person is so mean, or when we don't understand the circumstances, it is easier sometimes to say, "That's just the way it is," or, "That's just the way they are." Sometimes we say that because we don't want to get involved; it might require something from us. Let's put some effort into this and find out what's really going on. Maybe we should do some research into the situation or ask questions to find out why the people are the way they are. Sometimes it can be as simple as that. Sometimes we can get to know a person better and understand their attitudes and some of their actions simply by asking questions and gathering some data. Often, we may find that there is something in their lives that desperately needs prayer.

I had a coworker who was always grumpy; he was a royal grouch. It seemed he was always in a black mood, and nobody enjoyed talking to him because he always had an attitude. One day, I got adventurous and asked him if he was feeling bad that day. Turns out, his wife was dying of cancer and he was having a difficult time dealing with it. I asked him if I could pray with him and after that, we became pretty good friends. Even though he was still grumpy at times, he and I formed a friendship bond; he was not grumpy around me anymore He knew that he could trust me to pray for him from then on.

Prayer is the most effective tool that we possess, and it works. God loves us and wants to answer our prayers. God loves the person who might need an attitude adjustment in our opinion. God can transform that person and change his or her attitude. God loves that person too and can change his behavior. There is nothing that our God cannot do. He is bigger than anything we can imagine. It is God's desire to heal all of us because he loves each of us so much. Also, we can more effectively share his love with others if we are healed in body, mind, heart and spirit. If we are praying and are not in the will of God, we need to go to that point again where we are in the will of God. Then we can pray according to his will, and our prayers will reap success. Being in constant fellowship with Jesus through our daily prayer lives and studying God's Word will enable us to appropriate God's will in our lives more successfully.

You should also believe that it is God's will to help you prosper. God wants you to be healthy, wealthy, and wise. Even though he knows our needs before we ask, he still wants us to be dependent upon him as our Father, provider, healer and our God—our everything.

There is a great deal of evidence in God's Word that he wants to bless all his people. God is not a respecter of persons; he loves us all.

Having tenacity like a bulldog is not a bad thing when it comes to prayer. There is a story in the Bible in which one woman went to the king repeatedly, asking for the same request again and again, until finally, he grew tired of her constant asking and he gave in to her request. In Luke 18:2–8, Jesus told this parable about an unjust judge:

> There was in a city a judge, which feared not God, neither regarded man; and there was a widow in that city; and she came unto him, saying, "Avenge me of mine adversary." And he would not for a while; but afterward he said within himself, "Though I fear not God, nor regard man: Yet because this widow troubleth me, I will avenge her, lest by her continual coming she weary me." And the Lord said, "Hear what the unjust judge saith. And shall not God avenge his own elect, which cry day and night unto him, though he bear long with them? I tell you that he will avenge them speedily. Nevertheless when the Son of man cometh, shall he find faith on the earth?" (KJV).

This story is an example of how we need to persist in our prayers. I believe that God hears us the first time we ask for something, yet some things require that we ask more than once. Some prayers require that we fast and intercede. When we pray daily, we need to be sure to ask God to implement our priorities. We must be able to set up priorities before we can follow them. Once we have established a set of priorities that needs to include ourselves, our relationship with God, our families, our churches, our country, our states, our cities and our spiritual leaders, then we can pray effectively.

We should also ask God to help us live out the priorities that we—me and God or you and God—have established for our lives. Worshiping God goes a long way toward setting you up for a peaceful heart full of joy and allows you to enter into your prayer time before God with thanksgiving in your heart and a gladness to share time with God through your prayers.

It is at this point in your time with God that you should be able to ask him for the needs you want to present to him, remembering to always be thankful for what he has already done in your life. In your daily renewal or prayer time with God, you should be able to ask God to show you ways the things in your life need to be changed to better glorify God. You need to ask God to resolve those things in your life that require change or alterations.

You should never just accept things that are a negative influence in your life or the lives of your family members as "just the way they are." Your prayer can change things.

Who Is Your God?

There are so many names in the Bible for God. At a Bible study recently, we reviewed some of the ones from both the Old and New Testaments and what they meant. These are listed here:

Names of God:

1. Elohim: My God, my Creator (Genesis 1:1)

2. Jehovah: My Father (Genesis 2:7)

3. Jehovah El Shaddai (Genesis 17:4)

4. Adonai: My Lord, my master (Genesis 18:3)

5. Jehovah Jireh: My provider (Genesis 22:8)

6. Jehovah Rophe: My healer (Exodus 15:26)

7. Jehovah Nissi: My victory (Exodus 17:15)

8. Jehovah M'Kaddesh: My sanctifier (Leviticus 20:7–8)

9. Jehovah Shalom: My peace (Judges 6:24)

10. Jehovah Tsidkenu: My righteousness (Jeremiah 23:5–6)

11. Jehovah Rohi: My shepherd (Psalm 23)

12. Jehovah Shammah: The Lord is there (Ezekiel 48:35)

We all like to be referred to by our names—usually our first names or using a salutation like Mr. or Mrs. With our last name. Some of us even have extra names—nicknames—some of which refer to personality traits, much like those of God. There are accepted methods of addressing one another and using the name that is most common. It is my contention that God likes to hear his own names whenever we are speaking to him too. That should not be too difficult, considering the fact that there are so many names we can use for him: the Great I AM, Prince of Peace, our shepherd, our provider, our peace, and many, many more including the ones named above.

Perhaps it would be appropriate to use the name that is most conducive to our request at the time we are talking to him. For example, prior to getting married, I would respond to Miss Spraberry or Rhonda Honda, Freckles or Strawberry, depending on who was speaking to me. After I was married, I preferred to be called Mrs. If we need to speak to our heavenly Father and we are desperately in need of peace in our lives, I think it would be appropriate to call him by the name Jehovah-M'Kaddesh—Jehovah is peace. If you are in need of financial help and that is the basis of your request, maybe you could apply the name Jehovah-Jireh, meaning "God's provision shall be seen," to your prayers.

Most of all, whether we have the names figured out or not, our Father God wants to have an intimate relationship with us. I heard a definition of the word *intimate*— "into me he sees." Above all else, he wants to hear his name on your lips, like a lover likes to speak the name of his or her love. He wants you to call on his name, whichever name you may choose.

Whenever I need guidance, I know I can go the great shepherd—his name is Jehovah-Tsidkenu—and ask him for guidance in a decision about how to handle a seemingly impossible circumstance or situation and for help in dealing with a difficult coworker, customer, or family member. He will give me the right words to say, or he will tell me the right way to handle something by giving me a small idea that works.

Our pastor's wife recently told a story illustrating her message, in which she said, "What if Jesus was sitting at your kitchen table, waiting to visit with you and have an intimate time with you—just waiting on you?

"What if you saw him sitting there, waiting on you to have time to fellowship with him, and you were just so busy going about your daily chores and the business of life that you never took the time to sit down and relate the things in your life and share them with him? What if you did not ask him for his will and what he would have you do? What if you did not give him the opportunity to take care of some of the things in your life that were causing you to be so busy and stressful? What if you did not take the time to develop your relationship with him, not even when he was sitting there waiting on you? You were so tired at the end of the day that you didn't even take the time then to converse with him regarding your day or the next day."

That reminded me of a poem I retain in my home files. This was another one of those things that someone emailed to me years ago and I have no basis for the author's name or when it was written. It goes like this:

"What If?"

God couldn't take the time to bless
us today because we couldn't take the
time to thank him yesterday?
God decided to stop leading us tomorrow because we didn't follow him today?
We never saw another flower bloom because
we grumbled when God sent the rain?
God didn't walk with us today because
we failed to recognize it as his day?
God took away the Bible tomorrow because we would not read it today?
God took away his message because we
failed to listen to the messenger?
God didn't send his only begotten son because he
wanted us to be prepared to pay the price for sin?
The door of the church was closed because
we did not open the door of our heart?
God stopped loving and caring for us because we failed to love and care for others?

God would not hear us today because we
would not listen to him yesterday?
God answered our prayers the way
we answer his call to service?
God met our needs the way
we give him our lives?
Author Unknown

This poem was emailed to me and some friends at work one day years ago by a nonbeliever who thought I'd enjoy the poem. For me, it was powerful—not just a poem, but a wake-up call.

What if God were to cut us off from him because we weren't willing to communicate with him daily and maintain a prayerful, word-filled, Spirit-filled relationship with him?

Whatever you call God—Lord, Father, Jesus—as you pray, just know that his love for you does all the things listed in the above poem and so much more. Why? Who is God? God is love—love in the purest form and a form that someone who does not have a relationship with God couldn't begin to understand.

Recently, in my daily devotion, I was reading some of the beautiful books in Proverbs, and one thing I noticed was how often those verses mentioned our mouth and what we spoke; they emphasize how powerful our words are. God created this world by speaking it into existence, so he must place a high value on words, right? Words can heal, and words can wound. They can also be tools to pray God's will into people's lives, and they can then begin to implement change in people's lives.

Never say "never." This applies to praying for people too.

Another phrase that could apply here is, "Don't give up." God will answer your prayers. It's possible that he might answer your prayers using different methods than you had hoped or expected, and sometimes the answer will not be what you wanted; but if you are praying within the will of God and allowing him to guide you, you will more often than not find him answering your prayers in a positive way. God is such a loving God, and he is crazy about you and having a relationship with you. He loves you that much.

Sticks and Stones

Words are so important. Many times, you determine things that occur in your life by your mouth. Are you in the habit of speaking blessings or curses? It is too easy to fall into the habit of having a negative attitude, especially whenever it seems that your life has nothing going for it and that everything that could possibly go wrong in your life has. The problem with that is that you have been deceived. Yes, that is Satan's job, or did you forget he's out to kill you? It's his job to try to destroy you and me. If he can, he will convince you to give up your life one way or another, either through speaking curses over your own life, having you believe the curses that someone else has spoken over you, or even convincing you that your life is not worth anything anyway—that there's no use in living. He will try to kill you using any method, idea, emotion—anything he can use to try to keep God's truth and God's promises from being manifested in your life. He knows that there's great power in God's Word and in God's promises to all of God's children, including you.

Have you ever heard that child's saying "sticks and stones can break my bones, but words can never hurt me"? Oh, that we were all that strong! I remember we used to say that a lot to one another as children in our neighborhood when someone called us a name we didn't like. It was a fairly common saying among the youth at that time. However, it's not true. Our words *do* have power; they even have the power of life and death in them. Sticks and stones will break our bones, but words can break our hearts, our spirits, and our self-esteem. Whether we are small children, unable yet to speak out for ourselves, or whether we are adults, mature in age, words still have the capability to hurt if they are misused or abused.

If you don't believe me, just listen to this story that I read in a 2004 issue of *Women's World* magazine. A young lady was diagnosed with cerebral palsy when she was a baby. When she was placed in a regular school, she was determined to excel and endured the horrible words of the other children all throughout her years in school; even some teachers and principals did not believe she was capable of achieving a diploma. Do you know something? She had a balance that far outweighed those people who lacked faith in her—her mother. Her mother's words of encouragement and supportive attitude were sometimes all the positive influence she had in her life to keep her going. Her mother continued to voice her faith in her by encouraging her to keep going forward, telling her how smart she was and letting her know that she was capable of acquiring a degree if she chose to do so.

This young lady now has a master's degree and is happily married. There was a point in her life when she became very discouraged and pondered if she should just give up her efforts and accept the curses that other people had spoken into her life. However, the encouragement she received from her mother—those encouraging words, hugs, and that loving attitude of faith through her mother's love—lifted her out of the oppression that occurred when she was constantly barraged with negativity.

Her mother's words inspired her to continue to do the best she could. Wow! Just imagine what could have happened if she had been the victim of the discouragement that was directed to her. Our words have that much power; they can redirect others' lives, as well as our own. We can all learn a lesson from this young lady. Most of us don't even have the additional handicap that this young lady had; most of us are physically capable of doing what we choose to do, yet a lot of us have not accomplished half of what this young lady has. Perhaps we have not had such a wonderful, loving and encouraging influence. Perhaps we did not have parents whose words inspired us to keep on. We are living in the here and now, however, and we can change the path on which we are walking—switch to a more positive track. How? By speaking those positive words over our own lives. Do not accept the lies of Satan because in the end, God wins.

We could all be encouraged just by hearing positive words applied to our own lives. Bless your life with the words you speak about yourself and what is happening in your life every day. Curses are negative words spoken about others or events that are occurring in their lives—like a negative prediction. Many times, people speak negative words about situations in my life, and I try not to let them sink in. I try very hard to negate their negative words by speaking positive ones myself. I would prefer to bless my life, as well as others' lives, than to speak negative predictions into others' lives. When we speak words of blessing or encouragement, we are capable of inspiring, encouraging, and uplifting others; we are speaking life into others' lives. Your words are so important.

> An anxious heart weighs a man down, but a kind word cheers him up.
> Proverbs 12:25

> A person's words can be a source of wisdom, deep as the ocean, fresh as a flowing stream.
> Proverbs 18:4

> The tongue that brings healing is a tree of life.
> Proverbs 15:4

Joyce Meyers stated that "encouragement costs you nothing to give, but it is priceless to receive." We are responsible for every word that comes out of our mouth—good or bad. I'd much rather be responsible for good, encouraging, life-giving words to everyone who crosses my path. Wouldn't you? Unfortunately, I cannot claim to always produce the fruit I'd like to in that area—yet. God's still working on this child of his, and he daily erects another wall within this structure he's constructing. As recently as this week, God gave me the opportunity to hear the words I was speaking to someone else through a child who repeated, verbatim, the words I was saying. That was an eye-opener. It served to make me want to choose to articulate only encouragement.

Sometimes it is not possible to speak encouragement. Sometimes we are required to speak the truth in love. At those times, I strongly believe that tact is required. When we need to reprove someone, using tact and filtering our words through prayer will more clearly show God's love. Johann Wolfgang von Goethe said, "Correction does much, but encouragement does more. Encouragement after censure is as the sun after a shower."

According to many teachings we have been hearing within our congregation lately, this is the time of the kingdom dispensation, a time when all seeds that are sown will be fully realized. It is my desire to sow seeds of encouragement, hope, and peace rather than to discourage or harm someone else. We are all God's favorite child, and who wants to offend or hurt God's favorite child? We don't want to have to reap the rewards for that, right? Small seeds grow into large trees and could provide shelter for someone in the middle of an emotional storm—someone who's trying to make some decisions and needs peace. I want God to use my seed for that kind of growth, don't you?

Here's another famous Proverb- 12:6, which I'm sure you've heard before: "The speech of the upright rescues them"

Proverbs 12:18 says, "And thoughtless words can wound as deeply as any sword, but wisely spoken words can heal."

I don't know about you, but I want to be rescued when I require assistance. I do not want to speak words that will jeopardize that possibility, do you? I would like to be wise enough to speak words that can heal someone in dire need of healing. Let's try to dwell on the positive things in our lives, as we have been told to do in Philippians 4:8, so that we can have the words that come from our hearts to our mouths be ones that will accomplish that goal. It all starts from within. I've always been known to use the mantra when speaking to my children, "If you can't say something good, just don't say anything at all." There have been times when I have had to clamp down my lips and say nothing at all in certain situations because nothing positive came to mind to speak. Once I got this mantra into my head and heart, it became a part of me; I got it. I truly believe that all the positive input we have been able to inject into our brains will stabilize our thinking and balance our attitudes in our lives.

I also believe that everything good in our lives comes from God. Some people would be quick to say that God sends the bad too, but I do not believe that. I do believe that many times, we bring on our own problems by making poor decisions, and we sometimes reap the repercussions of our actions. I believe God allows things that we have set in motion to come to completion so that we can learn from them. If we choose to participate in activities we know God does not approve of, we have to pay the consequences by reaping what we sowed. Living with attitudes of rebellion or depression will cause us to act out of those attitudes.

God wants us to experience all the good life has to offer because we are his children, just as normal, earthly parents want to give all the good to our children. However, we all have to learn to deal with the negative events in life without allowing them to overcome us, and we need to be able to remain in a positive state of mind. One way to do that is to be thankful for everything God has placed in your life, from your children down to your shoestrings. Speaking positive words over your life and being thankful help us to realize the good things that God has given to us.

Proverbs 21:23 says, "He who guards his mouth and his tongue keeps himself from calamity." This comes straight from God's Word; it is not just something I made up to fit in with my message. How much more proof do we need than that? I also believe that this verse ties in with my previous statement: if you can't say something positive, keep your mouth closed. If we will try to find the positive in everything that happens in our lives, we will be able to deal with less frustration and keep from causing others pain, confusion or stress. I realize that not everything that occurs in our lives will inspire faith and hope to spring up within us, yet there is always some little positive thing in every situation. I'm just saying look for the good in everything.

I keep a list of positives with me all the time. It is a list of things and people I am thankful for. When Satan tries to discourage me—and he does try very often—or begins with his lying campaign, I usually remember to pull out my list of positives and reread it as many times as it takes to help me get to the place where I can start to be thankful and begin to praise God for those items on the list. It's an odd list; it includes such things as my children and stepchildren, grandchildren, Christian parents, my upbringing, my pastors, chocolate, shrimp, Wild Cherry Pepsi, salvation, puppies, babies, kittens, etc. It's grown throughout the years, but it is simply a list of things I can thank God for, and it always works. When I look at that list, it usually doesn't take long to find the positive things in life and begin to thank God for them. That pulls me out of the negative thoughts and keeps me from accepting Satan's lies about me and my life. There are times when I have been tempted to believe Satan's lies—sometimes it's just easier to give in—but God is greater than anything Satan can put before us.

Angry words never seem to do any good either. This is one area I dealt with daily for years. I worked at a car dealership and found that people are not always as truthful, honest, kind, or caring as I would like for them to be. Big surprise. One thing I always knew was that at some point during the course of the workday, someone was going to be angry or disappointed that they even had to get their vehicle repaired or by how much something costs.

In the past, I was known to respond in kind. This is an area in which God continues to work with me daily. I must admit that occasionally I still slip. However, since I have been trying to work on this aspect of my life, you must know Satan continues to try to get me to release words of anger in my responses to angry or upset people. One thing God taught me was to slow down—slow down my thinking and my response time and ask for God's help before I respond to their anger. I ask God to show me how to respond and to guide me and not allow me to say something that I may regret. Words spoken in anger are almost always regretted, and it is not possible to take them back. Once you have spoken a word, it is out there and continues to live on and on. Sometimes words hit a mark in a person and can really hurt. Wouldn't it be better not to toss out the angry words in the first place? I believe if we will slow down our responses—be slow to anger—we will learn to practice the power of peace. God help us all to be able to put the power of peace into practice in our lives more often.

Just as encouraging, uplifting, and positive words have a powerful impact to help others, words of anger have the ability and power to hurt. I don't want to place myself or anyone else under the negative power of anger. I would much prefer to see us all through the eyes of peace, with encouragement and kind, loving, uplifting words. I believe that God expects that from us as his children as a practice in learning how to love one another. He truly loves each one of us, including the homeless person on the street. Once we get that true concept into our heads, it's much easier to love everyone, not just select people in our lives—everyone. I also believe that the moment someone walks into our churches, that visitor should feel God's love so strongly that it will immediately attract them to Jesus. It is our responsibility to create that kind of atmosphere through practicing our love for one another and our love for God and extending that love outside of the church building and into our communities. How else will someone who needs to come to Jesus be encouraged to come to him if we are not showing the love of God? How else will they see anything different within us that will make them want what we have and make them want to become Christians and live for Christ?

I believe it is our responsibility to practice the power of peace through kindness, love, and encouraging words that lift up others. That is one act of love. Love is not just a noun. It's not an idle thing. It is an action verb, and it's a verb I believe I thoroughly discussed in my first book, *Journey of Love*.

The words we use are a reflection of many things about us—the words we use to speak to our children, for example. Our children are totally dependent upon us, their parents or caregivers, at the beginning of their lives. When a good relationship exists, throughout their entire lifetimes they are dependent on us for word support. The first words a baby hears are those of its mother during the pregnancy and throughout the child's infancy. The words of that parent or caregiver who is in constant contact with the child are the words that help to form the child's ideas, character, sense of humor, sense of self, and knowledge of God. They even help to form the inner thoughts of that young person based on the words with which they are nurtured throughout their growth to maturity.

Words have made or broken people in the past. Kind words have been known to lift a person's spirits, and kindness spoken to another is giving life to someone else. Once you have spoken a word, it cannot ever be taken back; it can only go forward. Let's try to share encouraging words with everyone we meet in our lives and give them words of life, not death.

Captive Thoughts

A lot of times, we allow the enemy, Satan, into our lives. We allow him to tell us about our lives because we don't call on God's Spirit. We have to remind Satan what God has spoken over our lives. Remember; Satan is the snake of deception; deception is his game, and believe me, he's been at this game a long time and knows how to play it and how to play you. He goes after you right where you will hurt the most. If he can make you forget those things that God has spoken over you—God's Word and what it says about you, your life, your ministry, your gifts talents, abilities, etc.—then he will convince you that nothing good is going on in your life and that you are a nobody. He will try to tell you that you don't matter to anyone; that nobody cares about you. He will try to deceive you into believing that you have no authority to impact the world, the church, your family, and your community.

How do you think so many people are persuaded to commit suicide? Where do you think depression comes from? Satan has convinced people who struggle with these problems that they do not matter to anyone. We are joint heirs with Jesus Christ; that means we do have power—the power to call on the name of Jesus Christ and the power to call on God's Spirit to come and take over any situations in our lives that appear to be impossible.

God is still in control, and he knows what's going on. We cannot allow Satan to deceive us into thinking that whatever circumstances we are involved in—whatever the situation—that God is not there for us or that the situation is bigger than God. Nothing is bigger than God. We can do all things through Christ Jesus who strengthens us (see Philippians 4:13). Greater is he who is in us than he who is in the world (1 John 4:4–5). God is greater.

Our proof is in the Bible—God's Word. We have to delve into it, and we have to learn it and allow it to soak into our hearts. We must keep our thoughts under captivity, under control. How do we do that? By thinking about those things that are good, those things that are pure. We must renew our minds as in Ephesians 4:23–24, which refers to a renewal of spirit in your mind. Put on your new man, a new paradigm, and a new way of thinking. Don't practice "stinking thinking"—negative thinking. We can pray and call forth the Spirit of God in our lives. God tells us who we are; Satan tells us who we are not.

How often have we been known to say, "I can't do this," or, "I can't handle any more?" Well, we have been convinced by Satan—his job is to deceive—that we cannot handle one more thing. Satan would like nothing better than to drag us down into depression by being able to convince us that we cannot do something or handle any more.

See 2 Corinthians 10:5, which reads, "Casting down all thoughts that exalt themselves, rather than exalting God."

We must be submissive to God's authority; the enemy, Satan, must even submit to God and to God's Word, but if he can get you so depressed that you allow his words to become your reality, then you won't bother to call on God. He will discourage you and encourage you to wallow in self-pity and distrust God. If you get to that place, you will have no desire to read your Bible, pray, or ask God for help.

You do have authority in your life, however. We all deal with a certain amount of depression or discouragement at times in our lives, but we don't have to be bogged down by it and stay there. We can be lifted out of it by praising God. Praise always works for me. We are joint heirs with Christ, and, as a result, we do possess the authority to take control of getting out of those types of situations. We can call on the Holy Spirit to lift us out of that place of negative thinking. We have the authority to overcome moods that do not glorify God and that produce negative lifestyles.

Anything that causes you to have shame or condemnation does not line up with the Word of God; therefore, it is not of God and not from God. Guilt is a natural byproduct of sin; however, condemnation is not. Condemnation can be felt by others who consider themselves to be above your sin, but it still comes from Satan. Shame is not in God's plan for your life; forgiveness is.

I'm told that often, depression is a result of sin in our

lives that has not been resolved. If you tend to be depressed a lot, maybe it's time to examine your life and find out if there might be a root of sin lingering there that needs to be dealt with. John 5:25 says, "Hear God's word, and choose life."

If you are going through shame and condemnation and choose God's Word to speak, do not accept any condemnation from Satan. If you have issues in your life that are sinful and need to be dealt with, God is there and willing to forgive you. Just ask him, and he will.

I am referring to Satan trying to limit what you are able to do for God by belittling your capabilities and making you think that you can't do something God has given you the gift to do. God has equipped us all with gifts, abilities, and talents, and he will complete the work he has started in each one of us, thereby giving us the abilities to accomplish his will for our lives. God has not placed those limits on anyone.

Satan wants you to feel disabled, crippled, ineffective, too shy, clumsy, stupid, unable to do things, ashamed, ugly, and not good enough. Why? Because then you might not call on God and allow God's Spirit to lift you up out of that depression.

Philippians 4:13 reads, "I can do all things through Christ Jesus, who strengthens me." Speak the Word over your life whenever you feel that depression or sadness—however you would describe that feeling coming over you. Do not listen to Satan telling you who you are not; listen instead to God's Word, which says you can do all things through Christ Jesus. Speak that word over yourself instead of allowing Satan's negative words to influence your mind into believing a lie. If something does not edify or build you up, then it is not of God. Condemnation is not from God. Where else would it come from? Satan—the deceiver.

Transform your mind by speaking blessings over your life. If everything doesn't always seem rosy, then don't dwell on those things with negativity. Instead, speak God's blessings over your life by speaking the good, concentrating on the good, and by being thankful for all the good in your life. Bless your own life. If there is something in your life that doesn't exalt God, don't get depressed about it; do something more positive about it. Confess it to God. Ask for his forgiveness, and leave it there. He will handle the rest.

Even the world has to bow down to Christ, as illustrated in Philippians 2:9–11, which says, "Wherefore God also hath highly exalted him, and given him a name which is above every name: That at the name of Jesus every knee should bow, of things in heaven, and things in earth, and things under the earth; And that every tongue should confess that Jesus Christ is Lord to the glory of God the Father." Your circumstance must bow down to God. We must proclaim with our mouths by speaking the Word of God over our lives. The Bible has many references to our tongues and our mouths. Even though the mouth may seem like a very small, insignificant part of our bodies, it is the rudder of the ship; it guides the ship. If we are not careful, we can get into deep waters very easily. We should call forth the Holy Spirit in our daily lives by speaking the Word of God.

Psalm 18:45 reads, "Let the God of my salvation be exalted." Let my life exalt the Holy Spirit—our Father

God, Jesus Christ—in my home, my work, and in all of my life, no matter what the situation or set of circumstances.

How do we keep our thoughts under captivity? Ephesians 4:20 says, "Let no corrupt words come out of my mouth." Don't speak death and corruption into your life. Speaking negative thoughts starts putting things into motion. Speaking positive thoughts also creates motion. Speaking death and corruption into your life pulls down your foundation, making it crumble. When vocalizing positive thoughts, dreams and hopes for the future has begun—when it starts to roll along and picks up speed— it creates positive results in our lives. I have already spoken to you in this book regarding the way our words affect our children and everyone who is touched by our lives. We are also affected by our own words. Speak life to yourself as well as others. Your blessings are not dependent upon your circumstances. Regardless of the circumstances, continue to do what God has told you to do. Read his Word, and speak his Word over your life, don't believe the liar, Satan. He wants your negative speaking to bring you into depression and disable you from speaking blessings over your life. He doesn't care if you have to suffer and experience physical, emotional, and spiritual pain unto death. That's his goal. Remember, his job is to steal, kill, and destroy, and if you give into his destruction of your life, he's happy; you are one more human he has convinced to forego living for God.

Instead, exercise your faith. Give it muscles by daily working it out by speaking good things over your life, even when it doesn't seem they will ever happen. Go ahead—think and speak positively what God's Word says about you. What does God's Word say about your situation? See James 3:5–12 which says that your tongue has the power to affect your life. We cannot control our tongues if our hearts and minds are not submissive to God. In order to get to that point, we must read God's Word, pray, and have the Spirit of God quicken God's Word so that we can hide it in our hearts. This means we need a very intimate relationship with God daily. Whenever we have hidden God's Word in our hearts—when it is needed either to encourage someone else or to help us get through a situation—it will come forth as needed. Deposit the Word of God like you would deposit money into a savings account. When it's time for a withdrawal, it will be there.

Remember, it is Satan's goal to discourage you, but you don't have to accept that for your life. You don't have to believe him; you have other options. Yes, I know that sometimes our circumstances are bad, but God is there for us. If you have the full armor of God, you have a powerful team on your side. Remember to put on the full armor of God each morning, and you will be better equipped to face those situations with peace and security in the knowledge that God is in control and will take you through it. Situations may not dramatically change, but you will have more peace, and just knowing that it will not last forever will help you get through. When you asked God into your heart, the full armor of God was made available for your use. Exercising your faith, learned by reading God's Word, and allowing the Holy Spirit to guide you will certainly bring about discernment, understanding, and peace in your life.

Just know also that you will need to be on the offensive rather than the defensive; God's armor covers the front of you. God is our rearguard also. It is our responsibility as Christians to stand and attack. We should not always have to defend our faith; we should be able, at some point in our Christian walks, to stand up for God—to pursue God through every method available to us. Greater is he who is within us than the one who rules the world. God is greater.

Offense is action: reading the Word and praying fervent, sincere, and heartfelt prayer. It is intercession: listening to God when he speaks to us and allowing the Holy Spirit to guide us. It is keeping our thoughts under captivity by dwelling on the good things God has placed in our lives. These are the actions of a great warrior of God. Nobody—not Satan, nor anyone alive—can tell you who you are. God is the only one who can do that. Do not believe the lies of Satan. You can do all things through Jesus Christ. Never say never.

I Just Don't Get It

Mark 8:34–36 says, "And when he had called the people unto him with his disciples also, he said unto them, Whosoever will come after me, let him deny himself, and take up his cross, and follow me. For whosoever will save his life shall lose it; but whosoever shall lose his life for my sake and the gospel's, the same shall save it, for what shall it profit a man, if he shall gain the whole world, and lose his own soul?" This verse is also found in Matthew 16:24: "Then said Jesus unto his disciples, If any man will come after me, let him deny himself and take up his cross, and follow me."

To me, these verses indicate that if we are willing to lose our lives for Christ, then we'll find them through Christ. Jesus knew that his followers would have to deny themselves in order to be able to follow him. He knew he would suffer and die and that he would also rise again. He taught his disciples in those three and a half years that they were following him—walking with him, ministering with him. Every day during those three years, Jesus taught them and told them what to expect when he died and rose again. However, they just didn't get what he was telling them.

Do we get it? Jesus died for us—for each one of us. He took everything on his own back when he suffered through all the beatings and took each one of those stripes on his back for you and me. What does that mean to us personally? It means that we can call on the name of Jesus for healing. It means that God must have loved us a great deal to allow his Son to go through all that—the hatred that became rampant through the group rage effect, all the humiliation that was heaped upon Jesus during that horrible time, and the unbearable physical pain.

As a mother, I find it difficult to even listen to someone criticize my children. I cannot imagine how God felt enduring the hatred and humiliation that Jesus suffered or the pain that was inflicted upon him in order to go to the cross so that you and I could have the opportunity to come to God through the blood of Jesus. God cared so much for us that he provided an easier method for us to come to him rather than having to go and sacrifice an animal each time it was necessary to speak to God. At that time in history, you could not just go straight to God without sacrificing an animal and having the priest go into the area called the holy of holies to pray on your behalf. God cared so much for us that he wanted it to be easier for us to communicate with him—to have a more intimate relationship with him.

Now, all we have to do is to accept Jesus into our

hearts—believe in him and become saved. After that, we have immediate access to God. We can access God at any time, day or night, because we have been covered by the sacrifice of all times—Jesus's blood that was shed at Calvary for us. I just don't get it. It is so easy for us now; why don't more people try it?

What's not to get, right? I don't get how we can possess this knowledge and not act on it. I just don't get how we can feel the pain of Christ when it's depicted in a movie or television show and not get that Jesus really does care about us and loves each one of us so much. Why is it so hard for us to lay down our lives for one another and show one another the love of God? Why is it so hard for us to admit that we need God in our lives? What is it about us everyday, regular humans that makes it so difficult for us to get it? We think sometimes that having faith in God has to be a huge, difficult task in order to accomplish our goals. It's been my take that it's just too easy for some people to comprehend.

Perhaps it is because we humans have souls where our natural lives are lived. If our emotions are out of order, then we are losing our souls. If we are not actively seeking the kingdom of God, then we are actively seeking after something else and are not allowing Jesus Christ to reign in our souls and in our hearts.

Matthew 6:33 reads, "Seek ye first the kingdom of God, and his righteousness, and all these other things will be added unto you."

Head knowledge is great, but heart knowledge is pre-ferred. If we gain the whole world and lose our souls, what good are we to the kingdom of God? The only kind of peace in the world is the peace of God, which surpasses understanding. That means it's a peace that even bypasses our souls, where we understand.

Anxiety can come through dealing with the things of our everyday lives; stress can come in and destroy our souls. If the soul is not prospering, we are not prospering. It's very possible that as Christians, sometimes we have learned how to make a living but not a life. Life flows through the love of God; life comes from God. Are we just going to go through the motions of life? Is it our goal to make sure that we have all the things that the world considers necessary or important for survival? Are we in survival mode? It is when we are not leaning on our Father God to lead us in our daily lives that we can lose our souls to the world. That is when Satan is able to step into our lives and acquire strongholds that can render our Christian lives ineffective. That can take over our lives without us even being aware that it is happening.

Suddenly, we have developed displeasing habits that are hard to break or quit, or we become dependent on something in our lives other than God. This could include anything from co-dependency in relationships to smoking, becoming dependent on prescription drugs, addiction to sex, pornography, and all other types of addictions. Please remember, these can happen to Christians too if we are not on guard and exercising our faith through putting on our armor of God daily. We all have to be very careful that we do not allow ourselves to become entangled in Satan's web of bondage, his web of lies. If we are dependent on a chemical to get through the day—drugs, alcohol, or anything that numbs the mind—how can we have a clear mind to be in a daily, intimate relationship with our Maker?

The only dependency in our lives should be upon God. If we are dependent upon anything else, Satan has a stronghold in our lives. If that is true, we cannot live effective lives for God. If our souls have been submitted to the Holy Spirit, then we can overcome those things that could become strongholds in our lives and live effective lives for Christ.

It is so important that as Christians we learn to be content with what God has placed in our lives. We cannot allow the things of the world to entice us to the point that we allow strongholds to develop in our lives. If we are so busy worrying about an addiction, then these items have a stronghold in our lives, but there is an outlet—a way out.

God wants to heal us. Jesus has already paid the price for our healing. Go to God, and he can and will gladly heal you from your strongholds. Give it to God, and allow him to deal with it. Some things require time for healing; others can be healed instantly. Many times, these things require some patience, growth, and much prayer to overcome, but we will overcome through Jesus Christ our Lord. God decides how and when to heal us. We have to practice our faith during that healing time, even if it takes a lifetime to heal. During the time that we are practicing our faith and waiting on our healing, we need to be using the God-given gifts we all have. As we give out what God has given to us, we will be healed. As we minister to others, we will receive. That's one of the benefits of giving when you are giving of your God-given gifts; you will always receive something in return. It could be healing or it could be the satisfaction of knowing that you are doing what God has called you to do.

Be content with what you have been given, and start to give out to others. Get past that "me, me, me" attitude and cultivate a giving attitude. Act out of your gifts, which may include baking a cake like nobody else can. You may be adept at writing poems or reading. You might be gifted in music, or you may be a budding artist. You may be able to write sympathetic notes or kind letters. You may have a gift of compassion. You may have a ministry of dance, song, or teaching—the list goes on and on. It does not have to be some huge gift for you to share with others; some of the aforementioned are not. My point is that whatever you are able to do for someone else, if you will focus on doing it for someone else as if you are doing it for Jesus himself, then you are giving to someone else a gift. That is what God wants us to do. This is what it means to lay down your life for another— to give up time that you would do something for your own benefit and give that time to doing something for someone else. That is actively loving one another—giving of ourselves to each other.

As your gifts are shared, they seem to multiply also. As you begin to give of your gifts, you will notice an improvement in the quality of your ability to perform that task or gifting. Excellence will come with the practice of your gift and in sharing it. It doesn't have to be some huge, sacrificial act on your part. It doesn't have to be a big showstopper like Billy Graham preaching or singing like Sandy Patty; maybe it's something as mundane as smiling at someone who needs a smile or just expending a kind word to someone who might just need to hear a kind word that day.

Be thankful for all that God has placed in your life. I've started to learn that being thankful leads to other fresh experiences in God, and it leads to other blessings. By loving various people throughout my church body experiences, I have learned that there are a lot of different kinds of people we can't begin to get to know in one short weekly church service. Getting to know people requires an investment of time. If you want to learn how to love someone, though—especially if you want to learn how to love everyone—then it will be necessary for you to learn how to separate the person from the enemy or from their words or actions many times. This means that you will have to learn to separate the physical being from the spiritual being. In other words, we will have to learn to dislike a behavior instead of disliking the person displaying that behavior.

Sometimes we find it is easier to judge someone than to separate the physical from the spiritual and dig deeper. We may not like the way they look, so we think we don't need to get to know them better. They might be a smoker who comes to church and smells like smoke so we'd rather not hug them—little things like that. If we will try, we will always find that God rewards the extra effort on our part. Many times, a new friendship is started by just going to shake someone's hand and spending a few minutes asking questions about him and his family, or by inviting someone to come back to your church for a special meeting they may not know about—a youth rally or special men's meeting on the weekend. Sometimes a bond can begin simply by sharing a smile. Investing a small amount of time in fellowship with another person can forge friendships for life, and many times, it opens up ways for the other person to come to Christ and be filled with the Holy Spirit. It draws them to you because of your friendliness, and then you have the opportunity to speak life into their lives. This has happened in my personal experiences before.

I just don't get it. Why don't we all try a little harder to love one another? Why don't we all practice sharing God's love with each other, especially those people who are a part of our daily lives? God loves each of us so very much, and I do believe this is part of what he expects from us as his children—that we share the love of God in every way imaginable and using every gift that God has given to us.

God's love is all you need. Putting God's love into practice in your daily life can be a big challenge, but I just don't get why more Christians don't try it.

I love you with the love of God. It is my prayer the words of this book have somehow brought comfort to you and that something will be gleaned from it that will assist you in your daily walk with Christ. Most of all, I pray that you will understand just a bit better how much Jesus loves you and how much your heavenly Father loves us all—that the Holy Spirit will lead you in the remainder of your walk with our Lord.

I want you to get it: God is in love with you. He wants to have an intimate relationship with you today and always. If you are reading this book and you have never asked Jesus Christ to be the Lord of your heart, I pray that you will do so now. He loves you so much. It doesn't matter what you may have done in the past or who you were in the past: he wants you, now and always. It doesn't matter how many times you may have slammed the door in his face. He will continue to love you and wants to have a personal, intimate relationship with you. Oh, how he loves you and me!

Thank you for reading my testimony and for sharing this time with me.